My Individualism
and
The Philosophical Foundations of Literature

Sōseki Natsume (1867–1916) is widely considered the foremost novelist of the Meiji period (1868–1914). After graduating from Tokyo Imperial University in 1893, Sōseki taught high school before spending two years in England on a Japanese government scholarship. He returned to lecture in English literature at the university. Numerous nervous disorders forced him to give up teaching in 1908 and he became a full-time writer for the *Asahi* newspaper. In addition to fourteen novels, Sōseki wrote haiku, poems in the Chinese style, academic papers on literary theory, essays, autobiographical sketches and fairy tales.

Sammy I. Tsunematsu is founder and curator of the Sōseki Museum in London, and the translator of several of Sōseki's works. He has also researched and published widely on the Japanese artist Yoshio Markino, who was a contemporary of Sōseki's living in London at the beginning of the twentieth century. Tsunematsu has lived in Surrey, England, for thirty years.

Sōseki Natsume

My Individualism
and
The Philosophical
Foundations of Literature

Translated by Sammy I. Tsunematsu

With an Introduction by Inger Sigrun Brodey

TUTTLE PUBLISHING
Boston • Rutland, Vermont • Tokyo

Published by Tuttle Publishing, an imprint of Periplus Editions (HK) Ltd, with editorial offices at 153 Milk Street, Boston, Massachusetts, 01209 and 130 Joo Seng Road #06-01, Singapore 368357

ISBN 0 8048 3603 5
ISBN 4 8053 0767 6 (for sale in Japan only)

The Translator would like to acknowledge the assistance of John Edmondson who kindly read through the English version and made many helpful changes.

Printed in Singapore

Distributed by:

North America, Latin America and Europe
Tuttle Publishing
364 Innovation Drive,
North Clarendon, VT 05759-9436.
Tel: (802) 773 8930; Fax: (802) 773 6993;
E-mail: info@tuttlepublishing.com
www.tuttlepublishing.com

Japan
Tuttle Publishing
Yaekari Building, 3F, 5-4-12 Osaki,
Shinagawa-ku, Tokyo 141-0032.
Tel: (813) 5437 0171; Fax: (813) 5437 0755;
E-mail: tuttle-sales@gol.com

Asia Pacific
Berkeley Books Pte Ltd
130 Joo Seng Road #06-01,
Singapore 368357.
Tel: (65) 6280 1330; Fax: (65) 6280 6290;
E-mail: inquiries@periplus.com.sg
www.periplus. com

This translation is dedicated to
Professor Nakashima Saikichi and Professor Nishi Tadaomi
in recognition of their warm encouragement and support.

OTHER TUTTLE CLASSICS
BY THE SAME AUTHOR

Contents

Introduction

A Crisis of Belonging

From his earliest years, Sōseki Natsume (or Natsume Kinnosuke, as he was born), experienced a series of crises concerning his sense of belonging and identity. The sad events of the first years of his life led to a powerful sense of dislocation that permeates his *oeuvre*. As we shall see in the important essays now available in English for the first time in this volume, his personal experiences led him to consider the philosophical and cultural significance of human isolation from a variety of perspectives. It is impossible to say whether Sōseki would have been as preoccupied with issues of isolation and belonging if he had not also lived in Meiji Japan—a culture obsessed with the issues regarding belonging and identity that arise from rapid change and dissociation from one's past. In any case, although a genius in his own right, the similarity between his individual concerns and the broader cultural concerns of the Meiji period enhanced the reception of his work and led him to become one of Japan's most important modern authors. His popularity is witnessed in contemporary material culture by the fact that Sōseki's face still circulates in Japan on the ¥1000 note—an honor that Sōseki might have declined, had he had the opportunity to do so, just as he declined many other public honors.

Sōseki's parents were upper-class administrators who found their social standing suddenly undercut with the fall of the feudal system, as the Tokugawa Shogunate collapsed. Partially because of their financial embarrassments, they gave their youngest son Kinnosuke to a local greengrocer. The green-grocers, busy with their daily work, neglected Kinnosuke, leaving him outside their shop in a basket. Finally, taking pity upon her young brother lying outside in the cold, one of Kinnosuke's sisters brought him home to his original parents. His parents gave him away again after a year, this time to a childless former servant named Shiobara and his wife. Domestic troubles eventually led the couple to divorce, and Kinnosuke returned to his original family. Kinnosuke, however, was unaware of his relation to his new guardians, thinking that his parents were more distant relatives. At age 21, he finally regained the family name Natsume, and a year later, adopted the pen name Sōseki, by which name he is commonly known today. His three successive families, the two aborted attempts to give him away, and his four name changes all lent considerable chaos to Sōseki's first two decades of life.

Sōseki's own life span (1867–1916) coincided almost exactly with the long reign of Emperor Meiji (1868–1912), and thus with the Meiji Era that witnessed unprecedented change in Japan. Sōseki's birth succeeded the arrival of Admiral Perry's "black ships" by only fourteen years. In 1868, when Sōseki was one year old, Emperor Meiji proclaimed his "Five Articles" that ousted the samurai from their seats of power, promoted Western-style education, and opened the door for a wide range of institutional and social reforms. The following decades witnessed a fascination with things Western, leading to sights that would have been unimaginable only a decade earlier. Alongside these cultural changes occurred the tremendous technological and industrial advances that transformed the Japanese economy and urban landscape. Sōseki lived to see the death of Emperor Meiji in 1912, and died four years later, in 1916. The events of Meiji left an indelible mark on him and others of his generation; all of his literary works reflect his preoccupation with the cultural and spiritual dangers associated with such rapid change.

Just as Sōseki moved from house to house as a young child and grew to be a stranger in his own home, not even recognizing his own parents, Sōseki describes the modern Meiji man as straddling cultures, dislocated both from Japan's past as well as from its future. This modern man, as Sōseki depicts him, has irreparably lost the innocence and moral integrity connected with Japan's neo-Confucian past, and is at the same time inexorably attracted to modernity, the West, and material success (c.f. Brodey and Tsunematsu, pp. 1–15). As a character says in his novel *Kokoro*, published in the same year as "My Individualism": "You see, loneliness is the price we have to pay for being born in this modern age, so full of freedom, independence, and our own egotistical selves!" In the two essays reproduced in this volume, Sōseki self-consciously defines the role of art and the artist in light of the loneliness and individualism of the modern world.

Redefining Japanese Literature for a Modern Age
Meiji literary discourse was not immune from the alternating waves of xenophilia and xenophobia that altered the terrains of other areas of Meiji cultural discourse. *Bummeikaika* (or "civilization and enlightenment"), a cultural movement encouraging rapid modernization and Westernization, made its presence felt

DATES	EVENTS IN SŌSEKI'S LIFE	PUBLICATIONS/ADDRESSES
1867	Natsume Kinnosuke born in Edo (Tokyo).	
1868	Adopted into the Shiobara family.	
1874–1878	Attends primary schools in Tokyo.	
1876	Shiobara step-parents divorce.	
1878–1884	Attends secondary schools in Tokyo; studies Chinese classics and English.	
1881	Natural mother dies.	
1883	Attends prep school, Kōtō Gijuku.	

DATES	EVENTS IN SŌSEKI'S LIFE	PUBLICATIONS/ADDRESSES
1884–1890	Attends the First Higher School, majoring in English.	
1888	Regains the name of Natsume.	
1889		For the first time uses the pen name Sōseki.
1890–1893	Attends the Tokyo Imperial University, majoring in English literature.	
1892	Joins the editorial staff of *Tetsugaku Zasshi*.	Writes on Laotzu and Whitman.
1893	Gains his BA from Tokyo Imperial University; enters the Graduate School of the University; appointed a lecturer of the Tokyo Higher Normal School.	Reads a paper on the concept of nature in English poetry.
1895	Accepts a position with the secondary school in Matsuyama.	Composes haiku poetry.
1896	Marries Nakane Kyoko.	
1896–1900	Teaches at the Fifth Higher School in Kumamoto.	
1897		Publishes "On *Tristram Shandy*."
1900–1902	Sent to England to study English; stays in London.	
1903	Returns to Japan; appointed as a lecturer at both the First Higher School and the Tokyo Imperial University.	Begins a series of lectures on English literature at Tokyo Imperial University.
1905		*I Am a Cat* begins to appear in *Hototogisu*; publishes *Tower of London*.
1906	Holds the first Thursday gatherings at his home; declines an offer from the *Yomiuri* newspaper.	Publishes *Seven Stories*, as well as *Botchan* and *Grass on the Wayside*; completes *I Am A Cat*.
1907	Accepts an offer from the *Asahi* newspaper to serialize his work; resigns from the	Publishes *Three Stories* and *The Poppy*, his first serial novel; delivers

DATES	EVENTS IN SŌSEKI'S LIFE	PUBLICATIONS/ADDRESSES
	Tokyo Imperial University.	"The Philosophical Foundations of Literature."
1908		Publishes *The Miner, Sanshiro*, and delivers "The Behavior of the Creative Writer."
1909	Declines the gold cup for being voted the most popular contemporary artist in the *Taiyo*; journeys through Manchuria and Korea; agrees to take charge of the *Asahi* literary columns; starts second literary column.	Publishes *Spring Miscellanies*, a series of personal essays, as well as *And Then, Literary Theory*, and *Travels in Manchuria and Korea*.
1910	Suffers a serious attack of ulcers.	Publishes *The Gate*; begins *Recollections*.
1911	Declines the government's Doctor of Letters degree; on lecturing tours, suffers an attack of ulcers.	Delivers "Entertainment and Professional Activity," "Modern Japanese Civilization," "Content and Form," and "Literature and Morality."
1912		Publishes *To the Spring Equinox*; begins *The Wayfarer*.
1913		After an interruption, completes *The Wayfarer*; delivers "Imitation and Independence."
1914	Suffers the fourth attack of ulcers.	Publishes *Kokoro*; delivers "My Individualism."
1915	Journeys to Kyōto, where he suffers another attack of ulcers.	Publishes *Inside My Glass Doors*.
1916	Dies on December 9th, following his last attack of ulcers.	Incomplete *Light and Darkness* published.

as Meiji authors tried to redefine Japanese literature, particularly Japanese narrative fiction, according to what were perceived as more modern (and Western) standards. The writings of one of the most influential revolutionary Meiji literary critics, Tsubouchi Shōyō (1859–1935), for example, forcefully promoted a shift toward tightly constructed plots with "logical development." In addition, specific Western authors and movements were chosen as particularly suitable for the new Japan.

Just as Meiji reform leaders attempted to inculcate European scientific method and rationalism through education reform, authors such as Shimazaki Tōson adopted Naturalism and the "scientific novel" from France as a mode suitable to the new level of scientific development in Japan. As a result, Naturalism dominated Japanese literary culture for the first decade of the twentieth century; in fact, it still has a strong presence today, just as it does in American fiction. Few Japanese authors, most notably Mori Ōgai and Sōseki, resisted this movement. In fact, Sōseki's dislike of Naturalism is one of the motivating forces behind both of the essays in this volume. In "Individualism," he examines the underlying Japanese "anxiety" behind the need to imitate the West that indirectly led to the excessive admiration for Naturalism. In "The Philosophical Foundations of Literture," he invokes examples from Zola and Maupassant, as well as Ibsen, to suggest the aesthetic poverty of a realistic depiction of sordid human conditions without the transforming power of beauty, virtue, heroic determination, or even attention to "technique."

Debates over literature in this same Meiji culture were thinly veiled discussions of national identity, particularly Japan's place in relation to its expanding world and the "West." As Etō Jun writes, "No matter how radically they differed from one another in their literary or political opinions, Meiji writers shared in the dominant national mission of their time: the creation of a new civilization that would bring together the best features of East and West, while remaining Japanese at its core" (Etō, p. 603).

Sōseki makes no secret of these two levels of discourse in the essays in this volume: each essay includes individual biographical anecdotes and also invites their allegorical reading as stories about the fate of Japan. Part of this tendency to allegorize his personal experience may stem from his painful awareness of his position as a representative of Japan during his two-year stay in England. It was one year after the influential publication of *Ukigumo*, Japan's first "Western" novel, that Sōseki became the first official student sponsored by the Japanese emperor Meiji to study English literature abroad. In "My Individualism," he mentions the burdensome responsibility he felt on this "unbearable" trip. In *Tower of London* (*London Tō*, 1907), he reports that "The two years I spent in London were the most unpleasant two years of my life. Among English gentlemen, I lived like a shaggy dog in a pack of wolves" (*Sōseki Zenshū*, XI, p. 10, IX, p. 14). After his return, Sōseki received his university position and became a prominent literary figure of the Meiji period, enabling him to help define the new direction of Japanese literature.

"My Individualism" gives us a rare account of his stay in London from the perspective of twelve years after his return, allowing us to see how Sōseki came to understand the profound shift in his thinking about literature that occurred during his stay there. In this essay, he recounts his irritation and sense of helplessness when Englishmen gave their opinions on literature, with which he disagreed. He suffered at not having his own sense of Japanese literature to lend support to his perceptions: "I had no hope of finding salvation if I did not formulate my own basic concept of what literature was." It is within the pages of the other essay in this volume, "Philosophical Foundations," that we find one of Sōseki's principal attempts to provide a cross-cultural framework for the interpretation of literature.

In the pages of both of these essays, we witness Sōseki's

reflections upon the pressures for modernization and Westernization in literature. The helpful combination of the two essays in this volume also allows us better to understand Sōseki's overall purpose. In creating a theory of literature that is characteristically Japanese, Sōseki wishes to provide Japan with its own literary discourse about the role of literature, satisfying its longing for Western-style philosophy or theory, its need to find a self-conscious approach to literature, and its anxious concern over national identity.

Literary Detours: Prefaces, Apologies, and "Ditches"

The first-time reader of "Foundations" might find the first part of the essay extremely abstruse. If one is not familiar with Sōseki's writing style, one can find oneself wandering in a desert of abstractions, longing for specific literary examples, and wondering whether one has made any progress toward understanding his central argument. It might help the first-time reader to understand that Sōseki's serpentine path of argumentation, his apologies, numerous prefaces, self-referential digressions, and even self-professed narratorial "ditches" are part of his self-conscious style and an attempt to combine elements of East and West. In fact, both his Japanese and British literary studies led him to prefer authors who focused on digressive, or "sequential," forms of narration (Brodey, pp. 193–9). Just as he was particularly interested in Laurence Sterne, whom he introduced to Japanese audiences in 1897, he was also influenced by the *shaseibun* tradition, championed by his poet-mentor Masaoka Shiki (1867–1902). *Shaseibun* showed a similar distrust of consciousness, rational control, and closure, and instead emphasized the idea of sketching verbal pictures from life, as in haiku.

Both of the essays in this volume originated as speeches. And in both cases, Sōseki revised them for serialized publication. It is interesting that in both cases, he chose to leave intact (or even emphasize) theatrical gestures of the speech, including direct comments to his audience and references to the passing of time, size of the room, etc. This is even more remarkable given that he informs us early on in "Foundations" that he has had to "almost double its original length" in order to make a comprehensible essay from his notes: "I was forced to rewrite my text completely." Despite the fact that these essays were written seven years apart, there are several similarities, particularly the opening preambles. In both cases, an illustrious institution offers a flattering invitation in person, Sōseki desires to (and attempts to) refuse the invitation, he reluctantly accepts, and finally he studiously avoids preparing for the speech, giving us frequent warnings of the poor quality of the speech to come. In the case of "My Individualism," he says he did not start writing it until the very morning of the speech; in "Philosophical Foundations," he refers to his meager "three or four pages" from which he will "talk wildly" to form his argument. His mock humility in these passages, obliquely drawing attention to his creative genius, is reminiscent of Romantic claims of unwitting or inspired composition, such as Coleridge's preface to "Kubla Khan" or Goethe's comments on the composition of *Werther*.

In other words, we have serialized essays that still maintain the surface appearance of speeches, for the sake of maintaining the non-linear, digressive style, as well as the guise of spontaneous order. Despite their revised and expanded character, Sōseki keeps using references to the historical speech in order simultaneously to provide humor and to excuse the gaps in argumentation. An example would be when he exclaims "the lecture has deviated from its main subject and has fallen into the very center of a muddy ditch. Let us quickly return and continue our progress in a straight line!" or "However, as I do not have time to explain this to you in detail, I am going to cut short my remarks."

Both essays, but particularly "Foundations," express Sōseki's disdain for traditional forms of social hierarchy, including the

precedence of university professors. Sōseki took the unprecedented step of renouncing his prestigious professorship at Tokyo
University in 1907, the same year that he published "Philosophical Foundations"; instead, he decided to publish his writings with the *Asahi* newspaper. And again, in 1911, three years
before the publication of "My Individualism," he once again
gained public notoriety for declining to accept the government's Doctor of Letters degree. His digressive style and references to the reverence in which professors are (wrongly) held,
help enhance his reader's sense that we are encountering his
own self-re-enactment. As readers, we are encountering his
literary personality in action. Sōseki wants his reader to understand that he is presenting perceptions rather than analysis—that
he is an artist rather than a philosopher.

Sōseki's extreme degree of self-referentiality can be surpris-
ing or annoying to readers, but also became one element of his
trademark style. Self is always at the center of his writings: at one
point in "Foundations," when he is about to "dissect" a passage
from Shakespeare's *Henry V*, he stops and suddenly decides to
"dissect his feelings" instead, because he says he understands
them better than the poem. Although by the end of this particular essay, Sōseki suggests ways in which we can transcend the
self through "correspondences" with readers (when we strike
sympathetic chords or ideals), our inescapable solitude and
therefore self-referentiality is at the core of his understanding.
The fact that identity issues are so central to all of his writings
is certainly one reason Sōseki's work resonated so well with his
Meiji audiences—and may also account for his popularity today.

Art Beyond Naturalism

"Foundations" begins with a strong statement of human isolation—the ailment for which literature provides a temporary
cure, or at least occasional relief. Human beings are in a state of
disunity seeking unity, or isolation seeking community. As we

discover by the end of this essay, human isolation and the temptations of solipsism drive the artist to art, and the author to write literature. Literature, if it succeeds in achieving "correspondences" with readers achieves a form of community.

To make his case, Sōseki posits a psychological model which includes three modes of mental operations that mediate the experiences of the senses and emotions (and that "originate from the ego"): namely, intelligence, perception, and will. While this model is far from complete, it helps us understand Sōseki's

LITERATURE AND THE IDEALS OF ART				
FOUR IDEALS OF ART	TRUTH	BEAUTY	GOODNESS	SUBLIMITY
Definition of the Ideal	Shedding light on "the human personality" through a "real object or the mediation of a real object"	The "representation of the emotions"	"The basis of virtue, fidelity, filial devotion, chivalry, and friendship"	Tragedy that displays grandeur, particularly the grandeurs of stoicism in the face of death; heroism
Mental "Operator" Involved in Ideal	Intelligence	[Preception] (Unclear whether operator is needed)	Perception	Will
Literary Examples of Ideal	Naturalism: Maupassant's "The Necklace," Ibsen's *Hedda Gabler*	Reference to "short poems" in contemporary Japan	None given	Two historical examples
Meiji Literary Status of Ideal	The dominant ideal in Meiji Japan	"Short poems"; otherwise "completely absent"	Not a popular ideal during Meiji times	Rare: "acts of heroism are more scarce in the contemporary world than at any other period of history"

sense of the place of the artist within the world of ideas. Different human activities, professions, and inclinations naturally give preference to one of these three mental operators, as he calls them. Those who "cause their intelligence to be exercised are people who have a clear understanding of our relationships with objects and beings outside ourselves; we normally call them scientists or philosophers." Will is the realm of many practical, active professions, such as "soldiers, politicians, tofu merchants or even carpenters." And while the man of letters must, according to Sōseki, also have both practical skills and philosophical skills, perception is his most defining characteristic: "People who exercise their perception appreciate relationships with objects or beings with enthusiasm." Through their perception, artists observe reality and transform it, endowing the world around them with feeling. Sōseki goes on to claim that there are four ideals by which we respond to the works of these operators, and according to which we prioritize them. These ideals are "Truth," "Beauty," "Goodness," and "Sublimity" (see chart, p. 19). In a work of art, for example, "one of these four categories will stand out more clearly than the others." These ideals, he says (though he never fully develops them in the essay), vary according to period, individual, society, and other contexts; therefore, moments in history can be defined by their dominant ideals.

The dominance of Naturalism in Japan, although never explicitly named, is in his thoughts as he developed this psychological model, and is in the back of Sōseki's mind whenever he mentions "Truth" and "Intelligence" in the body of the essay. For Sōseki, the artist exclusively devoted to Truth and who values only intelligence and not perception robs the artistic experience of part of its potential. Art, according to Sōseki, does not have to represent all four ideals, but can become misshapen: audiences can become "color blind" by an emphasis on one ideal that seeks to "actively attack and demolish another ideal." Naturalism's exclusive devotion to Truth, in other words, is pursued to the detriment of other ideals, impoverishing the literary experience.

As an oblique response to Naturalism's de-emphasis on style or "technique," Sōseki adds an interesting section where he compares two literary passages: one from Defoe and one from Shakespeare, one in prose and the other in verse. The meaning of the two passages when paraphrased seems equivalent, he argues, but their emotional impact, their involvement of the reader, and artistic quality differ greatly: Shakespeare's use of Etonymy and poetic condensation forces the reader to become involved in interpreting meaning, and thereby forces the reader into a participatory role in Shakespeare's creative process, allowing us to encounter a perceptive genius at work. Shakespeare "adjusts our spectacles to suit our vision," while Defoe's meaning is visible "with the naked eye" from "a long way off." Defoe's description "walks and drags its feet all year as if it had wooden legs"; it does not require imaginative participation from the reader or involve any poetic reconfiguration of reality.

The essay develops the psychological model in order to illuminate both the dangers of the current, "narrow" approach to literature by suggesting the broad spectrum of approaches that one can have. Part of his purpose is to inspire a new generation of artists to re-infuse art with the ideals of Goodness, Beauty, and Sublimity, by freeing them from the pressure of the single-minded devotion to Truth, from the attachment to Western fashion, and from the practical concerns of prestige and advancement. Sōseki culminates "Foundations" with a moving description of his ideal for art and the artist:

"If, through the continuity of awareness which we have discussed, a correspondence is established between our work and one person in a hundred, or even one person in a thousand, and if we have made a small contribution to the enhancement of Truth, Goodness, Beauty, and the Sublime, which will illuminate the essence of our work like flashes of lightning, we will leave traces difficult to efface. If, progressing even further, we are able to attain the ecstasy that produces the reducing influence—because the spiritual power of arts and letters can exercise a great and intangible influence on society—we will have fulfilled our mission by obtaining eternal life in the human story."

The Social Benefits of Solitude

Written near the end of the Meiji period, as Japan was reaching the zenith of its territorial expansion in Asia, Sōseki's famous essay "My Individualism" continues in his quest to liberate the Japanese artist toward such social goals, yet this essay resonates with a more sober sense of social and political dangers facing Japanese culture as a whole. Rather than focusing on the enthusiastic imitation of the West, Sōseki is now concerned with what happens when that imitative drive is converted into a desire for national or domestic homogeneity; when a mistrust of foreigners paradoxically leads to a mistrust of Japanese citizens.

Sōseki's concern is with a generalized "anxiety" or insecurity that may lead one to become either one of "Panurge's sheep" (part one of the essay) or a tyrant (part two of the essay). The slavish follower will be afraid to assert his own individual opinions or perceptions, while the tyrant will not allow others their own individual perceptions. These dual dangers, it turns out, have an element in common: they both involve an inability to recognize the separation of self from others. Ironically, then, the painful recognition of our fundamental human isolation, a recognition that provoked his earlier essay "Philosophical Foundations," serves in this later essay as the element of human existence best able to help us liberate ourselves and to allow others their freedom as well.

INGER SIGRUN BRODEY
Assistant Professor, Curriculum of Comparative Literature
University of North Carolina at Chapel Hill

Works Cited

Brodey, Inger Sigrun, "Natsume Sōseki and Laurence Sterne: Cross-Cultural Discourse on Literary Linearity," *Comparative Literature*, 50(3), 1998, pp. 193–219.

Brodey, Inger Sigrun and Tsunematsu, Sammy I., *Rediscovering Natsume Sōseki*, Kent, UK: Global Oriental, 2001.

Etō, Jun, "Natsume Sōseki: A Japanese Meiji Intellectual," *The American Scholar*, 34, 1965, pp. 603-19.

Natsume, Sōseki, *Sōseki Zenshū*, Tokyo: Iwanami Shoten, 1965.

_____, *The Tower of London* (trans. Peter Milward and Kii Nakano), Brighton: In Print Publishing, 1992.

My Individualism

This is the first time I have been in this Gakushūin. It is not very different from what I have long imagined it. However, what I was imagining was a little vague.

As Mr Okada so kindly mentioned in his introduction, he asked me last spring to give a lecture or something similar. However, something stopped me from doing so at the time. Mr Okada seems to remember the reason better than I, and I found the explanations he has just provided amply sufficient to clarify the situation. Whatever the case, I was forced to decline the offer provisionally. However, not wanting to be rude, instead of refusing outright, I offered to give the lecture during the following session. This time, to be on the safe side, I asked Mr Okada when that new session would take place. He replied that it would take place in October this year. Then, mentally calculating the number of days left between April and October, I told myself that I could easily find something to say since I had so much time. "That suits me," I said, thus confirming my agreement. However, luckily or unluckily for me, I don't know which, I fell ill and was confined to my bed all through September. When October arrived, the month to which I was committed, I was no longer bedridden, but I was still unsteady on my legs and I would have had difficulty in giving a lecture. On the other hand, I could not ignore the promise I had given and the thought that someone would pester me some day to fulfill it was a source of anxiety.

The unsteadiness in my legs soon disappeared, but the end of the month arrived without my receiving any news of the lecture I was to give at the Gakushōin. It goes without saying that I had not told anyone about my illness, but, as two or three newspapers had broached the subject, I thought that my situation was probably appreciated and that a replacement had been found. This thought reassured me. Then Mr Okada suddenly appeared before me in flesh and blood. He was wearing boots for the purpose (of course, the fact that it had rained that day had something to do with it). He came right to the edge of the Waseda district to give me the following message: the lecture was postponed to the end of November, by which time he was sure I would be able to keep my promise. As I had assumed that I was excused from the commitment, I was, I admit, somewhat taken aback. However, there was still a month left, and I told myself that I would easily find something to say. So I responded to his suggestion by renewing my agreement with him.

In light of what I have just told you, you will assume that between last spring and October, and then between October and November 25th, I had enough time to find enough ideas to make up a coherent lecture. But I was unwell and thinking about such things was painful and stressful for me. So, until November 25th arrived, I did not worry about it and lazed around. The days passed, one after another. Finally, when there were only two or three days left and the deadline was near, I had a vague notion that I should think about preparing for the lecture. But this was such an unpleasant prospect that in the end I spent the day painting.

Perhaps you will think I have a talent for painting. In fact, I contented myself with scrawling childish things on the canvas; I put the picture on the wall and spent a couple of days contemplating my work and daydreaming. Yesterday—yes, I think it was yesterday—someone came to see me and told me that my painting was very interesting. More precisely, it was not the picture itself that was interesting, but it was like something else I had painted when I had been in an exceptional frame of mind. I told my visitor I had painted the picture not because I felt happy, but because I was sad.

I began to explain my state of mind: just as certain artists bubbling over with happiness paint pictures, do calligraphy, write poetry or prose, others, because they are in the midst of cares and worry, take a brush to do calligraphy, paint a canvas or compose a work of literature, hoping in that way to attain happiness. Although it may seem strange, when we look at the results of these two different psychological states, we realize that they are often identical. However, although I am taking advantage, completely incidentally, of this occasion to point out this phenomenon to you, it is irrelevant to the subject I have chosen for my lecture. I will not therefore pursue it. So, anyway, I contented myself with looking at this strange picture and passing the time without worrying about preparing for my lecture.

Finally the 25th arrived—the day I had to appear in public and give my lecture whether I wanted to or not. So this morning I have tried to bring together my ideas a little, but I feel that I am inadequately prepared. As this lecture will not leave you completely satisfied, with this prospect in mind I ask you kindly to be patient.

I do not know when your club began its activities, but personally I do not see any problem in your calling on outside people to give lectures. However, looking at it from another point of view, it seems to me that, whoever you invite, there is not much chance that you will hear a lecture that fulfills your needs. Is what interests you perhaps rather the novelty of someone from outside, someone different?

Here is an ironic tale that a Rakugo storyteller told me. Two noblemen were once hunting a falcon near Meguro. After riding about all over the place, they grew hungry. Unfortunately, no meal had been prepared for them, and as their servants were far away it was impossible for them to satisfy their appetite. The only thing they could do was go to a squalid farm nearby and ask the people there for something to eat. An old peasant and his wife, taking pity on them, grilled a samma, a sort of mackerel, which they had to hand and served it with rice mixed with barley. The two noblemen made a hearty meal of the fish and left the farm. The next day, the strong smell of samma lingered in their noses and they could not forget its delicious taste. So one of the noblemen invited the other to dinner and promised him a samma. The servants were astonished by the order, but as it came from the master, there was no question of opposing it. On their command, the cook, with the aid of a pair of tweezers, removed all the little bones from the fish one by one, soaked it in rice wine, grilled it and served it to the nobleman and his guest. But they were no longer hungry, and the ridiculous care which had been taken in the preparation of the samma had made it lose its taste. They took a few mouthfuls of this strange meal with their chopsticks, but it was failure. They looked at one another and said, "To savor a samma, we must go to Meguro!" These words, which may seem strange to you, are the conclusion of the story.

You who are in this excellent institution, the Gakushōin, are constantly in contact with excellent teachers. So now that a person like me has been asked to come and give a lecture, will you not, having waited from spring until the end of autumn for me, be disgusted by the delicious party dishes that are served here and would you not, consequently, like to taste the Meguro samma?

I see Professor Ōmori sitting in this room. We left university more or less at the same time—one year apart, I think. Mr Ōmori once told me that his pupils did not listen attentively to his lectures and that he found this irritating. They were also not conscientious and this was very annoying. I remember that his criticism was not of pupils at the Gakushōin but of those at some private school. I responded to him in a way that was, at the least, discourteous.

I am ashamed to repeat it here, but I said to him, "Is there, in any country anywhere, a student who wants to listen to your lectures or even those of anybody else?" Perhaps Mr Ōmori did not fully understood my point at the time, so I am taking the opportunity today to dispel the misunderstanding, if there was one. When we were students and were the same age as you— we may have been older—we were much lazier than you. It would be no exaggeration to say that we never attended the professors' lectures. I am, of course, only talking about my own experience and what my friends were doing: it may not apply to others. However, when I look back at the past today, it seems to me there is some truth in all this.

As for myself, I gave the impression of being docile, but I was not at all an attentive student: I just lazed about. With such recollections in mind, I never have the courage to criticize, like Mr Ōmori, the conscientious students I see today. And it was in wishing to express this feeling that I made such a thoughtless suggestion to Mr Ōmori. In coming here, I had no intention of making excuses for my conduct towards Mr Ōmori, but I am taking the opportunity to make amends to you all.

I have wandered off on to an unanticipated topic, so I am going to try to return to my speech.

You are in a famous institution. Famous professors are constantly guiding you in your studies. Every day you are taught by them, in general or specialized subjects. I suppose you have intentionally invited someone like me to come from outside and lecture to you because you wanted to try something new, exactly as the two nobles wanted to eat the Meguro samma. But in truth, I think that the lectures by the professors you see every day are much more useful to you and much more interesting than anything someone like me can say to you. If I were a teacher in this establishment, my suggestions would not be stimulating because of their novelty. Such a large audience would not be assembled and my lecture would not give rise to such enthusiasm, nor such curiosity, it seems to me. What do you think?

Why am I making such suppositions? Well, to tell you the whole story, many years ago I wanted to teach at the Gakushōin. It was not I who made the first move: a friend who worked here recommended me. At the time, I was a scatterbrain who had no idea what direction to take after university to earn my daily bread. Now, when you set out on life, if you just fold your arms and do nothing, the money to pay your rent does not simply turn up out of nowhere. I did not question whether or not I was qualified to be a teacher: it was absolutely necessary for me to fit in somewhere. When my friend told me he had recommended me, I got in touch with your school and took the first steps towards putting in my application. At that moment, another candidate appeared, but my friend told me that my application was going well and there was nothing to worry about. Thinking that my appointment was no longer in doubt, I enquired what a professor should wear. He told me that a jacket was necessary for classes, so, before my appointment had been confirmed, I ordered a jacket. At the same time, I had only a very vague notion of where the Gakushōin was.

It is very odd, but, when the jacket was ready and against all predictions, my application was refused. The other professor was chosen for the post of English professor. I have now completely forgotten his name, but the resentment I felt was probably not too intense: I think it was someone who had just come back from the United States. If this person had not been appointed, if I had become, by a stroke of luck, a professor in the Gakushōin and had taught here up to today, perhaps I would not have received your kind invitation and I would not have had the chance of addressing you from this platform. Does not the fact that you waited to hear my lecture from spring until November prove that, even though I failed to get into the

Gakushōin, you see something novel in me, as if I were the Meguro samma?

I should like to say a few words to you about what happened to me after my application to the Gakushōin had been rejected. It does not logically follow from what I have just said, but it is a very important part of the lecture I am giving today. I would therefore like you to listen carefully to my words on this matter.

I had been refused. I had nothing left but the jacket I was wearing. Apart from that, I had no other Western clothes. That was how it was! Where do you think I was going in those clothes? In those times, unlike today, it was very easy to find a job, probably because there was a lack of available employees at the time. Wherever I turned there were suitable vacancies. In my own case, I received two offers simultaneously: one was from First Higher Secondary School and the other was from the University Teacher Training College. I half agreed with the plan of my professor friend, who had recommended me to the Higher Secondary School, but at the same time I had thoughtlessly made polite inquiries at the Teacher Training College. So I was in a fine mess. I was young, so I made mistakes and was careless. It was clear that I would have to face the music, but I really did feel at a total loss.

I was summoned by my professor friend, an experienced teacher in the Higher Secondary School, who gave me a dressing down:

"You say that you are coming here. At the same time you contact another establishment. So I, acting as your intermediary here, am in a very difficult situation!"

Pushing stupidity to the point of anger, because I was young, I told myself it would be better to refuse both posts at the same time and began to take steps in this direction. Then I received a message from Mr Kuhara, who was at the time headmaster of the Higher Secondary School and is now president of the Kyoto University of Sciences. He asked me to go and see him at his institution. I hurried over and found the headmaster of the University Teacher Training College, Mr Kanō Jigorō, in his office together with my professor friend who had presented my application. Mr Kuhara informed me that an arrangement had been made: I had no need to be embarrassed as regards the secondary school and it was preferable that I should work in the Teacher Training College. Under the circumstances, I could not refuse and I replied that I would accept the suggestion, but I could not help feeling that I was in an irritating situation. I must tell you that at the time I did not think much of the Teacher Training College. Of course, when I think about this today, it seems completely unjustified.

Even though I was only meeting Mr Kanō for the first time, I tried to be evasive, saying:

"According to your own account you are looking for teachers to serve as instructors, to be a model to the students. I am completely unqualified for such a position."

Mr Kanō responded:

"You are a competent person. When I hear you reject my suggestion with such honesty, I want you to come and work with us even more."

He would not let me refuse the job, and, although I was not by nature an acquisitive type who would want to teach in two schools at the same time, I had caused trouble for several people through my lack of maturity. So in the end I decided to go and teach at the Teacher Training College.

However, it was clear at the outset that I did not have the qualifications to be a good teacher, and I am sorry to say that I was very ill at ease. Mr Kanō said it was a pity that I was so honest, and perhaps it would have been better if I had been more devious. However, I could not help thinking that the post did not suit me; to speak plainly, I felt like a fish out of water.

Finally, one year later, I was appointed to a college in the country. It was a college at Matsuyama,[1] in Iyo province. I see that you laugh at my mention of Matsuyama College. You have no doubt read my work *Botchan*. In that novel there is a character whose nickname is "Red Shirt," and at the time I was asked who this person might be. At that period, I was the only teacher who had a degree, so if we want to find real people behind every character in *Botchan*, well, it must have been me hiding behind "Red Shirt." I want to tell you that this is very lucky for me.

I lived in Matsuyama only for a year. The prefect asked me to stay there, but since I had already given my word to another establishment I could not accede to his request and I moved on to somewhere else. This time I went to Kumamoto[2] high school. Looking at it chronologically, I acquired my teaching experience at the college, the high school, and then at the university. I have yet to try a primary school or a girls' school.

I lived in Kumamoto for a long time. Then, I unexpectedly received a confidential note from the Ministry of Education. They were offering to send me to London for studies. I had spent quite a few years in Kumamoto, had I not? At the time I was thinking of refusing the offer: after all, I told myself, what use to the nation would it be for me to go abroad with no particular objective? However, the principal professor, who was the intermediary who informed me of the secret plans of the Ministry, said, "It is they who make the assessment. It isn't up to you to assess yourself. In any case it's best for you to go." So,

---

[1] A town on the island of Shikoku, capital of the province of Ehime, near the Inland Sea and the famous Dōgo springs.

[2] A town on the island of Kyūshū, near the east coast, on the Shirakawa River, and capital of the province of Kumamoto. It has a population of over 500,000. It is an ancient feudal town (house and gardens date from the sixteenth century) and a place of Buddhist pilgrimage. Near it is Mount Aso, one of the largest Japanese volcanoes.

as I had no reason to refuse, I obeyed the Minister's order and went to England. But as I had expected, I had nothing to do there.

To explain this to you, I must tell you what I did before I went abroad. The story I am going to tell you is part of the lecture I am giving today and I ask you to listen carefully.

At university I specialized in English literature. Perhaps you are going to ask me exactly what I mean by "English literature." For me, after three years of study, it was as hazy as a dream. Dixon[3] was my professor: he made us read poems and prose extracts aloud in class; he made us write essays; he snarled at us when we forgot articles, and got himself into a temper when we made mistakes in pronunciation. In the examination he asked us for the dates of the birth and death of Wordsworth, the number of pages in Shakespeare's manuscripts, and even a chronological list of the works of Walter Scott. That is the only type of question he set for us.

However young you may be, you can doubtless understand what I am saying. When I wondered what English literature was, and when I wondered first what literature itself was, temporarily leaving aside English literature, I of course had no answer to the question. If I had been told "You only have to read it yourself to understand!," I would have retorted that that would be like a blind man looking through a fence. I could not find anything in the library that caught my eye, however long I browsed over the shelves. This was not simply because of a lack of willingness on my part, but also because the available resources were poor in the field of English literature. In any case, I studied for three years, and at the end of it I had under-

---

[3] James Main Dixon (1856–1933) taught English literature at the Imperial University of Tokyo from 1886 to 1892. He was also the author of a dictionary specially designed for Japanese students, *Dictionary of Idiomatic English Phrase, Specially Designed for the Use of Japanese Students*.

stood nothing about literature. And I am forced to admit to you that this was the source of the torments I was to suffer.

I set out on my working life with this ambivalent attitude. Rather than say that I became a teacher, it would be better to say that circumstances led me into that profession. By good luck, as my linguistic skills were not strong, the different subterfuges I used every day managed to keep me out of trouble. However, in my heart I had a profound sense of emptiness. In fact, if it had been genuine emptiness, I would have been able to deal with it, but the deep dissatisfaction I felt, tainted with irresolution and ambiguity, was unbearable; to crown it all, I was not in the least interested in my adopted profession of teacher. From the outset I knew that I did not have the right temperament to be a teacher. Teaching in class already bored me. How could I help it? I felt turned in on myself, as if I were getting ready to disappear into my own world. But did that world exist, yes or no? No matter in which direction I looked, I didn't dare disappear anywhere.

"Since I was born into this world, I must do something in it," I told myself, but I had not the faintest idea of what was good for me. I remained paralyzed, like an isolated being surrounded by mist. I expected at least one ray of sunshine to penetrate the darkness, or, even better, I would have liked to have a searchlight so that I could see clearly before me. But a single ray would have been enough. Unfortunately, no matter where I looked, everything was indistinct, confused. I had the impression of being trapped in a bag which I could not get out of. "If I had a gimlet I could make a hole in this bag and escape from it," I thought, impatient in the extreme to get out of it. But, alas, no one gave me a gimlet and I was incapable of finding one myself. I spent dark days within myself speculating on what was to become of me.

In the grip of this anguish, I graduated from the university. Spurred on by it, I moved from Matsuyama to Kumamoto and then I left Japan with the same anxiety. As soon as you begin to study outside your own country you become aware of new responsibilities. I worked as hard as I could and did my utmost to achieve something. But, whatever book I read, I never managed to come out of the bag. However much I paced the city of London in search of a gimlet to rip the bag, I would never have discovered one, I believe. In my room in the boarding house, I began to reflect. The situation was absurd. "There is no point in reading all these books," I told myself, and then I gave up. I no longer saw any reason to read the books.

At that moment, I understood for the first time that I had no hope of finding salvation if I did not formulate my own basic concept of what literature was. Until then I had floated at random, like a rootless aquatic plant, relying entirely on the opinions of others. At last I became aware that I had reached an impasse. When I say that I based myself on the opinions of others, I mean that I was an imitator, like someone who makes others drink his liquor, then asks them their opinion on it and makes it his own, even if it is wrong. It must seem odd to you when I put it like this, and you may doubt that there are such imitators in reality. In fact, there really are.

Recently, Westerners have been talking a great deal about Bergson[4] and Eucken.[5] The Japanese also, behaving like

---

[4] Henri Bergson (1859–1941) was introduced to Japan by Kaneko Chikusui and Katsurai Tonosuke who translated *Creative Evolution*, published in France in 1907. The philosopher quickly became popular in the archipelago: we even hear of a "Bergson boom." Bergson was a spiritualist, and it is very appropriate to recall that his philosophy advocates "a conscious and considered return to information from intuition."

[5] Rudolf Euken (1846–1926), a German philosopher. His philosophy is based on a religious spiritualism of Christian inspiration (*The Share of Truth in Religion*, 1901). He influenced Max Scheler. A professor at Iena, he was one of the promoters of the idealist reaction against naturalist thought. He won the Nobel Prize for literature in 1908.

Panurge's sheep,[6] are making a good deal of fuss about them. In my time, it was even worse. If you came across any suggestion from a Westerner, whatever it might be, you adopted the point of view blindly and with great affectation. Whatever the occasion, people littered their speech with foreign words, recommended them to their neighbors, and considered themselves very intelligent in so doing. Everyone, or almost everyone, wanted to do the same thing. I am not maligning other people: in fact, I have behaved like this myself. For example, if I read a critique by a Westerner of a book written by a Westerner, I would spread the ideas all over the place, whether or not I understood them, not thinking at all about the proper merits of the judgement. I would stroll around arrogantly talking about some subject which was foreign to me, which was not in any sense my own, deriving from my own being. It did not worry me that I had swallowed it whole, and if I acquired knowledge mechanically, that did not bother me either.

Nevertheless, however much people praised me because I was strutting around wearing other people's clothes, deep down inside me were the early stirrings of anxiety. I wore peacock feathers easily and strutted around proudly, but I began to understand that if I did not abandon the borrowed plumes, that if I did not go back to something more authentic, the anxiety within me would never disappear.

For example, a Westerner may well say that a poem is magnificent, that the style is remarkable, and that is his opinion as a Westerner, even if I happen to mention it. If I did not agree, I was not obliged to adopt his ideas. I was an independent Japanese. I was never the servant of England. As part of the Japanese nation, I owed it to myself to make my own judgement. Besides, from the moral perspective—in which honesty is

---

[6] *Jigasaren*, private soldiers, carrying a rifle; subalterns; servile partisans without influence, Panurge's sheep.

central and a virtue that is prized by all the countries in the world—I had to stay faithful to my personal opinion.

That, however, does not prevent me from specializing in English literature. I found that I generally became annoyed when I disagreed with the ideas of a native English critic. I had to ask myself what was the cause of the disagreement. Was it due to a difference in customs, feelings or habits? If we went deeper into it, we would attribute this disagreement to national character. But the average scholars, confusing literature and science, would conclude that what suits country A could not but give his admiration in country B, and would be seriously mistaken. I must say that I myself was mistaken on this point. If I find it impossible to reconcile myself with English critics, I must be able to explain why. Simply by formulating this explanation, I can throw some light on the world of literature. At the period I am speaking of, I understood this for the first time. That was extremely late. But it is the straight truth, and I will not distort the facts for you.

From that moment, in order to support my positions in relation to literature—in fact, it would be better to say in order to develop new convictions—I began to read works which had nothing to do with great literature. In short, I ended up pondering on the expression "self-centered"[7] and, to test this concentration on myself, I plunged into the reading of scientific and philosophical works. Now times have changed, and people who have any sense at all must understand the problem I have been talking about. But at that time, I had the intellectual level of a child and the world around me was hardly more advanced. In fact, I had no other way out.

I gained a great deal of strength from this period of introspection and it prompted me to ask who these Westerners were.

---

[7] This concept of concentration on oneself (*Jiko hon i*) is opposed in a dualist binomial to "concentration on others" (*Ta-nin-hon-i*).

In fact, this concentration on myself set me in motion—I who up to then had remained stuck in one place, disorientated—and pointed out the way to me.

I must admit that this marked a new departure in life for me. When we imitate Westerners and make a lot of noise about nothing, it only brings us anxiety. So if I endeavored to explain to people why they should not let themselves be thus influenced, telling them it was better that they should not act like Westerners, not only would I feel I was doing the right thing but they too would benefit greatly. That is what I thought. Then I decided to dedicate my life's work to carrying out this plan by writing books and in other ways.

At that moment, my anxiety disappeared completely and I began to explore the city of London with a light heart. To put it metaphorically, my pickaxe had finally struck a rich seam. Let me add, at the risk of repeating myself that the path I had to take, which until then had been shrouded in mist, was now clear to me.

By the time this light dawned within me, more than a year of my stay in England had passed. It was impossible for me to accomplish my plan while I was still abroad, so I resolved to collect as much material as I could and to complete my work when I returned to Japan. By pure chance, I would return to my country with a strength that I did not have when I left it.

However, as soon as I arrived back in Japan, I had to take steps to ensure that I could earn a living. I started giving lessons in a Postgraduate School and I also taught at the university. As this still left me without enough money, I also worked in a private school. To crown it all, I lost my nerve and I was forced in the end to publish trivial articles in magazines. Because of the burden of these various tasks, I had to abandon a project that I was halfway through. *The Theory of Literature* that I had published seemed not so much to represent the work I wanted to accomplish as to be the remnants of a defeat. It was like a deformed child, or, rather, it was like the ruins of an unfinished city which had been destroyed by an earthquake before it had been completely built.

However, that idea of concentration on myself, which appeared at the time I have spoken of, never left me for one moment. Indeed, as the years passed, it grew stronger. The plan to create my life's work had met with failure. However, the conviction that I acquired at that time, that the Ego is the essential ingredient and that others are merely secondary, brings me today great self-confidence and a deep feeling of peace. It seems as if this is what allows me, even now, to continue to live. In fact, it is perhaps thanks to this strength that I can stand on this platform and give you this lecture.

Up to now, I have really only summarized my experience for you, but, in an excess of concern for you, the idea behind my story is that you should identify in it some relationship to your own situation. You will all leave this establishment and go out into the world. For many of you, this will not be for some time; several of you will soon start to work in society. But I presume that you are all likely to repeat my experience; that is to say, you yourselves will feel the same anguish that I once endured (even if it is of a different nature). I think there must be many among you who are very angry because you want to find an opening somewhere but cannot; you would like to grasp something firmly but you grip only a smooth bald head.

If some of you have already found an opening in some way, you must be exceptional cases. There are also those who satisfy themselves by following a traditional path, and I would not say that there is anything wrong with that, if it brings them inner peace and confidence in themselves. But if you have no support, you must go on whatever the cost until you reach the place where, as you dig with your pickaxe, you discover a seam. You must go on, because if you do not find the seam, you will spend all your life in an uncomfortable situation, treading water, not knowing what to do. If I lay so much stress on my own example, it is so that you will not be plunged into perplexity: it is not in any way to propose myself as a model. However normal I may seem, I know that I have managed to make my own way, and if you think my way is absurd, your observations and criticisms will not harm me. I think that I am satisfied with the path I have chosen, but let there be no misunderstanding between us! This path has given me satisfaction and peace of mind, and has enabled me to have confidence in myself, but I do not at all believe that, because of this, the path that I have followed can act as a model for you.

In any case, I can certainly detect in you the same type of anxiety that I experienced. Is that true? If it is, ten years, twenty years, sometimes a whole lifetime will be needed to find something tangible at last. "There it is! I have finally found the way that I should follow! I have finally reached my destination!" When these exclamations are yours, you should find peace of mind. When you utter these words, an infallible confidence in yourself will make you hold your head up high. Perhaps a number of you have already reached this stage. But if there are some among you who are tormented by the mist and thick fog that have risen in your path, whatever sacrifice you are driven to, you will be satisfied, I think, when you reach your destination. It is not a question of working only for the good of the country or of your family; it is something that is absolutely essential for happiness.

If you have already taken a similar path to mine, what I have to say will be of little use to you, but if any obstacle appears in your path you must overcome it, or otherwise, regrettably, you will fail. Of course, the mere fact of going forward does not mean that you have taken the right direction. There is nothing else to do but walk until you find something tangible. I have no desire to remonstrate with you, but as I think that your future happiness depends on this process, I cannot remain silent on the subject. I am giving this speech because it seems to me that it would be unpleasant for you to find yourselves in a situation where you felt like you were floating between two currents, with your nerves as weak as sea cucumbers, making you completely irresolute and preventing you from understanding your problems in depth. If you tell me that it is not unpleasant for you to experience such a state, then I have nothing to add, and if you tell me that you have successfully passed through this unpleasant trial, that is also very good. I pray with all my strength that you will pass these tests successfully.

However, as far as I am concerned, after I left university I did not manage to extricate myself honorably from this situation until I was thirty. Obviously this caused me inevitable suffering, and it persisted year after year. That is why, if anyone among you is affected by a condition similar to my own, I cannot help hoping with all my heart that he will valiantly follow his chosen path. I permit myself to say this because, when you reach your final destination, you will finally discover a place of which you can say, "I can truly rest peacefully here!"; you will have peace of mind and you will gain confidence in yourself for your whole life.

What I have told you up to now constitutes the first part of this lecture. Let us now embark on the second part. The Gakushōin is generally considered to be an institution that receives people who have the benefit of a comfortable social position, and that is certainly the strict truth. If, according to my assumption, the great mass of poor people do not enter this establishment but, rather, children from good families, or from the upper classes, are assembled here, the first thing that is appropriate to mention, of all the aspects of your life in the years to come, concerns the exercise of power. In other words, when you get a job, you will clearly have more power at your disposal than poor people.

I said earlier that you must persevere until you reach, thanks to your efforts, a destination that brings you happiness and peace of mind. However, why do we thus strive for happiness and peace of mind? Well, in all probability, you will reach that stage when you find your chosen way and find yourself for the first time confronted by your individuality, which has been yours since your birth. Once you have found your path, if you pursue it with determination your individuality will develop little by little. When your individuality and your professional activity are in perfect harmony, you may say for the first time that you are satisfied with your life.

When I analyze this notion of "power," which I mentioned, I realize that what we call "power" is an instrument that allows us to infiltrate ourselves to some extent into the head of some-one else. If the fact of describing power as an "instrument" seems too blunt to you, let us say that is something that can be used as an instrument.

The power of money accompanies power in the strict sense of the term. It is inevitable, ladies and gentlemen, that you hold this power too, and in a much more clearly defined manner, than poor people. If I look at the power of money within the same framework that I used to analyze power in general, well, this seems to me to be an extremely useful instrument in enlarging the field of one's own individuality by seducing or suborning others.

We must thus consider that power in general, and the power of money, are extremely useful instruments which allow those who possess them to impose their own individuality on others or to cajole others to go in their desired direction, and they can do this with infinitely more ease than poor people. Those who have this strength may seem to be remarkable people. In fact, they are extremely dangerous. I have already told you that, in the general context of studies, literature, "liberal arts" and leisure, individuality can develop only when our Ego has fulfilled itself. However, to be frank, the application of this principle can be effected in a wider sense and is not limited to the arts and sciences.

I know two brothers: the younger is happy to stay in the house and read books, while the elder is a fanatical angler. The timorous behavior of the younger brother, who does nothing but shut himself up in the house, disgusts the elder brother profoundly. Finally, believing that his brother has been steeped in misanthropy because he does not want to trouble the fish, the elder drags the younger off on a fishing trip. The sport deeply displeases the younger brother and he finds it intolerable. However, as the elder brother pushes him to accompany him to the fish pond and to carry the fishing rods and basket, he gives way, hoping that he will not catch anything. However, he spends the day pulling roach out of the water against his will and returns home completely disgusted.

Did the younger brother's character change as the elder envisaged as a result of his action? Not in the least! It merely led to an extreme aversion to fishing. In short, the elder brother and the sport suit each other: no mismatch breaks the established harmony. This is what we call the individuality of the elder brother. The younger brother is completely different. This story is not meant, of course, to provide an example of the exercise of financial power: it is intended merely to explain how you can use your power to constrain someone else. Because of his individuality, the elder brother oppresses his younger brother and obliges him to go fishing against his will. Obviously, sometimes, when you take courses, when you are a soldier or when you are instituting strict discipline in an establishment, well, in these kinds of situations, it is impossible to avoid the use of coercive means to a certain extent. But I am going to talk of the time when you will be left to your own devices, when you will go out into the world. I should like you to listen to what I say, in case you find yourself in difficulties one day.

Let us imagine for a moment, as we have already said, that

you have the good fortune to come upon something that seems good to you, that you love, and that is in accordance with your personality. You go on and develop your own individuality, and then you forget to make the distinction between others and yourself and you feel the urge to bring someone into your camp, even if you have to force them in. At that moment, a relationship is established which resembles the one between the two brothers. Furthermore, if you also have the power that money confers, you will spread it around and you will try to force others to accept your image. Using money as a means of subjugating people, you can get others to change by force of seduction, leading them to act according to your will. People who do this are very dangerous!

This is what I have always thought on the subject. First, my dear audience, you will be unhappy all your life if you do not manage to settle peacefully into a professional activity that suits you and through which you can develop your individuality. However, if society allows you to obtain the respect that should be shown towards your individuality, is it not also completely correct that you should recognize the individuality of others and respect their inclinations? This seems to me not only essential, but also fair. Regarding it as unforgivable for others to turn left when you choose right would be silly, I think. Of course, when we are talking about complex subjects, such as Good and Evil, vice and virtue, some proper analysis of the problem is essential, even if it is only slightly developed. But when such complicated questions have not been raised and the problems do not require such careful attention, the following conviction seems inevitable: as long as others guarantee us our freedom, we must guarantee it to them under the same conditions and treat them as equals.

Lately we have talked a lot about Ego and awareness of one-self, using these terms to describe the self. We must recognize that there are many serious dangers. Some people, while insisting that we rigorously respect their Ego, take no account of the Egos of others. I am firmly convinced that if we look at things fairly and if we have a sense of justice, as we develop our own individuality to attain happiness we must at the same time guarantee to others the same freedom as we grant to ourselves. Unless we have reasonable cause, we must not be in any way an obstacle to the development of the individuality of other people, in their own way, allowing them to attain happiness. Gentlemen, why do I talk of being "an obstacle"? Well, I am sure that in future many of you will be in positions that will enable you to stand in the way of the freedom of others. Among you there will be many who will exercise power or will have access to large amounts of money.

To tell the truth, the exercise of power separate from the concept of obligation should never exist here on earth. As long as I exercise the right to make such propositions as I look at you from up here on this platform while forcing you to listen to me for an hour or two, it seems to me that I am offering you words to keep you quiet. Even if my lecture is second-rate, I must show dignity in my behavior and appearance, and that alone will make you show me some respect. In fact, I know that it could be said that you should behave fairly submissively because you are welcoming me and I am your guest. However, this is purely a matter of etiquette: it is simply a question of conforming to conventions and it has nothing to do with anything on the spiritual level.

I should like to give you an example. It must happen sometimes in class that your professors reprimand you. No? But if a professor exists here on earth who does nothing but reprimand his students, he clearly has no aptitude for teaching. To make up for his reprimands, a professor must put a great deal of effort into his teaching duties. A professor who has the right to reprimand his students has, as a consequence, the duty to teach. A professor often uses this right that has been granted to him to maintain discipline, is that not so? But if, in return, he does not fulfill the inseparable obligations that come with this right he should relinquish his duties.

The same is true of the power that money confers. Every wealthy man, in my opinion, must understand the meaning of responsibilities. I will explain what I mean to you very briefly. Money is something that is extremely convenient. We can use it as we wish in an infinitely varied way. For example, if I make 100,000 yen on the stock exchange, I can have a house built, buy some books, or even cheer up some geishas with the money. Money can be changed into anything we choose. And amongst all the possible choices, it can be used as a means of buying people's minds. Is this not frightening? In other words, by spreading their money around, people can use it as an instrument for purchasing the moral sense of others and so cause corruption and degradation of the soul. If that money we made on the stock exchange was to have such a great impact at the level of morals and ideas, I think that we could not fail to conclude that it would be an inappropriate use of it. We may think so. However, in fact, money circulates and we can do nothing about it. The only way the corruption of human nature can be avoided is if those who are wealthy spend their money with an appropriate ethical sense and do not use it to the detriment of moral principles. This is why I insist on saying that the power that money confers must be accompanied by the notion of responsibility. Today, there are people who do nothing but hold on to money. What I mean to say is that it would be extremely regrettable for others if these people did not strive to be aware of the precise purposes behind their spending, and of the consequences it entailed and the social effects of a particular use of money, and if they did not use their wealth in a responsible way. It would not only be regrettable for others, but it would also be unforgivable in the people themselves.

Summarizing my talk up to now, there are three key points.

First, when we talk about perfecting our individuality, we must take account of that of others by considering and respecting it. Second, if we intend to use the power that we have, we must be clearly aware of the obligations that are inherent in it. Third, when we want to exercise the power of money, we must emphasize the responsibility that is part of it. Those, in summary, are my three conclusions.

In other words, we could say that if we do not reach a certain level on the speculative and conceptual plane, the act of developing our individuality, manifesting our authority, or even using the power which money confers does not have the least value to enjoy these three privileges fully. It is essential to be directed by the humanity in our personality, and that humanity should underlie these three items. If our personality is flawed and we choose to develop our individuality inconsiderately, we hinder others. If we want to make use of authority, we abuse it. If we use the power that money gives us, we corrupt society. Extremely harmful events arise from these actions and attitudes. Gentlemen, in the future you will have ready access to these three privileges, so, above all, do not fail to become outstanding people, with real personality.

I am going to change the subject a little. As you know, England is a country that venerates individual freedom. There is no other country that loves freedom as much while still maintaining order. To tell the truth, I do not like England very much, but in spite of this, I must allow it one thing, reluctantly: probably, in no other part of the world, are the people both as free and as policed. Japan, for example, cannot claim to compare with it. But the English are not only free: from childhood, society inculcates in them a love of freedom and, at the same time, a respect for the freedom of others. For this reason, their notion of freedom is accompanied implicitly by the idea of duty. Nelson's famous words, "England expects that every man will do his duty," are not limited in their significance to the context of the period. They reflect a firmly established conviction that has developed in strict association with the idea of freedom: duty and freedom are two sides of the same coin.

When something upsets the English, they often organize demonstrations. The government does not get involved in these protests at all: it keeps quiet and takes no interest. And however often the demonstrations are held, the organizers understand the situation and do not encourage acts of disorder and violence that could embarrass the government. For some time, we have read in newspapers, or other publications, articles about the movement called the Suffragettes,[8] whose members commit acts of violence. But these are exceptions. Although there are far too many of them to be written off as an aberration, it seems to me that we cannot consider them other than an exception. Perhaps they can't find a husband? Or perhaps they can't get a job? Or perhaps they are taking advantage of the respect for women that has been inculcated in people for so long? All I can say is that this does not seem to me to be the normal behavior of the English. When the Suffragettes clamor and deliberately provoke disruption, destroying treasured works of art, going on hunger strikes in prison and causing trouble for the warders, and chaining themselves to the benches in the House of Commons, these are exceptional events. Perhaps they act so improvidently because they feel that men, faced with the problem of how to react, will be uncomfortable about taking measures against them. I do not know. However, whatever their reasons, it seems to me that they are an anomaly in the system. I think, as far as the ordinary temperament of the English is concerned, and as we have already said, their love of freedom is integrated with their concept of duty.

---

[8] Women who campaigned in England at the beginning of the twentieth century for the institution of women's right to vote. The election of John Stuart Mill marked the beginning of their struggle for female suffrage.

I am not suggesting that we have to take England as our model, but in short I do believe that there is no true freedom without the notion of duty. This means that a purely selfish freedom cannot exist in society. If it were to appear it would immediately be rejected by people in general, who would trample it under their feet. That is certain! Gentlemen, I hope you are free men. At the same time, I am eager that you should understand what the term "duty" means. I openly profess that I conceive of individualism as having this precise meaning and I will not hesitate for a moment to affirm it loud and clear.

There must be no misunderstanding of my use of the term "individualism." As it would be unforgivable of me to allow you, who are young, to misunderstand, please pay careful attention. Time is pressing, so I am going to try to explain to you what I mean by individualism as simply as possible. Individual freedom is absolutely essential for the individuality that I have described to develop. Since the development of this individuality will have a very significant effect on your happiness, it seems to me that we must establish a form of freedom that can be exercised without hindrance until it begins to affect others, a freedom in which I can go left and you can go right, a freedom which we can attain for ourselves and which we can concede to others. This, more or less, is what I mean when I talk about individualism. As regards the power and influence which money confers, in the same way, if we abuse it by saying to someone, for example, "I don't like your face; I'm going to beat you up!" or sending a chap to the other world because we have taken a dislike to him, or even in less serious ways, what happens then? When the individualism of people is destroyed, they are inevitably plunged into unhappiness. For example, if the Etōkyo Prefect of Police surrounded my house with police officers, without my having done anything wrong but simply because I might displease the Government, what kind of act would that be? Perhaps the Prefect of Police has the power to do this, but his moral sense would not allow him to abuse his authority in such a way. Well, let us suppose that, just because he detested me, a business magnate like Mitsui or Iwasaki bribed my servants and made them hinder me at every opportunity, how would we describe that kind of activity? If, behind their financial power, those people possess in any degree what I would call a "human" personality, they will never be drawn towards such crimes.

All such abuses occur because people are unable to understand the principles of individualism based on ethics. To satisfy their own interests, they try to expand their territory to their own advantage at the expense of the common run of mortals through either the power or the influence of money. But what I call individualism can in no way constitute a danger to the State, as the man in the street may think. According to my interpretation, the concept of individualism respects the existence of others just as it respects the existence of the self. These are noble ideas, I think.

If we put it more simply, individualism replaces political sectarianism with notions based on Good and Evil, Reason and Unreason. It recommends that we do act inconsiderately within political groupings or factions that favor the power or influence of money. Underlying these ideas is a solitude, of which others cannot be aware. As we do not belong to any faction, we only borrow, at our convenience, the path that we think we should take. At the same time, we put no obstacles in the way of others. Sometimes circumstances make it impossible for human beings to remain in harmony with one another, and that is when we feel solitude. Once, when I was responsible for the books page of the *Asahi* newspaper, someone whose name[9] I have forgotten wrote some unkind things about Mr Miyake

---

[9] It would seem that Morita Sōhei had replied in the *Asahi* of May 24th, 1910 to a criticism made of him in the *Nihon oyobi nihonjin* newspaper on May 15th about his private life.

Setsurei.[10] It goes without saying that this was not a personal attack: it was limited to literary criticism. Besides, it was only two or three lines long. I cannot remember when it appeared. I was fully responsible for the column, but perhaps I was not *au fait* with what was in it because I was confined to bed at the time due to my illness.[11] Or had I myself given the article the green light? That is very possible. Whatever the case, this criticism appeared on the books page of the *Asahi* newspaper and the editorial staff of the magazine *Japan and the Japanese*[12] were angry. They did not speak to me directly but asked one of my staff to withdraw the statement. It was not the main party, Setsurei, but his "performers" who took this initiative. The term "performers" is bizarre: it makes one think of a nightclub. Let us call them his colleagues. Well, they insisted that we retract completely. We would have done so, of course, if we had committed a material error, but this was a question of opinion and we could do nothing about it. I had no option but to insist that we were free to write what we wanted. Then certain writers in *Japan and the Japanese* began to malign me in every issue. This increased my astonishment even further. I did not enter directly into discussions with them, but when I learned what was going on from other sources, I felt very uncomfortable. That is to say, I myself was acting within the framework of individualism while they, on the other hand, were exhibiting sectarian behavior. This is, at least, how it seemed to me. At the time, I was going so far as to write adverse criticisms of my own works in

---

[10] Miyake Setsurei (1860–1945), doctor of arts, journalist and literary critic of a nationalist tendency. (See Kenneth B. Pyle, *The New Generation in Meiji Japan*, Stanford University Press, 1969.)

[11] One must remember that this was a critical period for the writer. On August 24th, 1910, he almost succumbed to a stomach hemorrhage.

[12] *Nihon oyobi nihonjin*. In April 1888, the Seikyosha publishers published the literary criticism magazine *Nihonjin*.

the books page for which I had assumed responsibility. So I was very surprised to see that they were angry simply because our criticism of Setsurei had displeased them. Their attitude seemed very strange to me. Please forgive my discourtesy, but to me it seemed an old-fashioned attitude in our contemporary context and it reminded me of the behavior of a corporation from the feudal period. In expressing this view, I could not escape a feeling of solitude which oppressed me. There are divergences of opinion among my closest friends, and I am well aware that nothing can be done about it. That is why, however much I may dispense advice to young people who come to me, I would never allow myself, unless there was a very good reason, to prevent them from expressing their ideas. I genuinely recognize the existence of others, and because of that recognition I grant them freedom. Whatever insult I may have to endure, I will never request the assistance of anyone who is unwilling to help. The solitude of individualism lies in this. According to these ideas, before we adopt an appropriate attitude towards another person, we first decide on the approach to be taken by assessing the situation in terms of Good and Evil. Thus we sometimes find ourselves completely isolated and experience solitude. It goes without saying that it is reassuring for twigs to be in a bundle.

I would like to add a word in order to avoid another possible misunderstanding. When we look at individualism, we consider it at first sight as ideologically opposed to nationalism; that is, it seems that it would by definition lead to the destruction of nationalism. However, there is no justification for this careless and unfounded interpretation. I do not much like such labeling: I think it impossible to classify a person in terms of his support for a particular ideology. For the sake of clarity, I am forced to talk about various subjects using the suffix "-ism." Some people spread the rumor that modern Japan will not survive if it does not embrace the theories of nationalism and firmly believe in those ideas. In addition, there are many who support the view that nationalism will perish if we do not attack individualism. These arguments are completely unfounded. In fact, we are at the same time nationalist, cosmopolitan and individualist.

Individual freedom is, without a doubt, at the heart of individualism, which serves as a foundation for the happiness of human beings. But this freedom rises and falls like a thermometer according to the prosperity or poverty of the country. Rather than speaking of this as an abstract theory, I would rather say that we have conceptualized reality. All things considered, situations develop according to the natural course of events. If the country is in danger, the freedom of the individual is restricted. In times of peace, freedom continues to develop. This process is quite natural. No one would concentrate on the thoughtless development of his own individuality, dissociating himself from these principles, if he saw that the country was threatened with annihilation. But the philosophy of individualism I am describing to you includes a warning to those who say it is essential to wear a fireproof helmet after the blaze has been extinguished, or that one should stay indoors when there is no need to do so. I will give another example. When I was at the high school, some of the pupils founded an association. I have now forgotten the details of it, what it was called and what it was for. In any case, it was a noisy club that displayed the flag of nationalism. Obviously, this society did nothing bad. It benefited from considerable support, including that of Mr Kinoshita Hirotsugu,[13] who was headmaster at the time. All the members of the club wore a badge on their chests. Although I was excused from wearing a badge, I was accepted as a member of the society. I was not, of course, one of the founder members and many of my

---

[13] Kinoshita Hirotsugu (1851–1910), doctor of law, headmaster of the First Higher School from 1889 to 1892. He then became rector of Kyoto Imperial University, and subsequently rector of Seoul Imperial University.

ideas were different from theirs. However, as I had no reason not to join the association, I became a member. Now, at the inauguration in the great amphitheater, and by I do not know what chance, a member got up on to the platform and started to harangue us. Although I was part of the company, as this member was to a large extent opposed to my opinions, I had already energetically attacked his views on the general aims of the association. Listening to the speech of this young man on the day of the inauguration, I became aware that he was refuting all my arguments. I do not know whether he was doing this intentionally or just by chance, but it was inevitable; I had to reply. So I could do nothing else but get up on the platform when he had finished his speech. I performed very badly that day, I think, but I was content to put my position laconically. Perhaps you will ask me what I said. It is really very simple: I stated more or less that the country was no doubt very important, but that there was no need at all to act the clown by talking about it all the time, as if one were completely possessed by it. There are perhaps some who say that we must think of nothing but the country, day and night, without end, but in fact it is impossible for anyone to think incessantly about anything. A soya pastry seller does not sell his produce for the good of the State. His basic aim is to earn something to make ends meet: that is why he does it. However, when we wonder if he makes a fundamental contribution to society, whatever his motivations, well, we can say that he is indirectly profitable to the country. In the same way, the facts that I have today eaten three bowls of rice at noon and that tonight my ration will be four bowls, are events that are in no way connected with the good of the country. To tell the truth, my habits are formulated so that my stomach works properly. We cannot deny that such things exercise, very indirectly, an influence on the outside world and are related, in a certain way, to the international situation. But as for the person who tells himself that he is eating for the good of the country, that he is washing his face for the good of the country, that he is going to the toilet for the good of the country, this is truly dreadful! I see nothing wrong in encouraging nationalism, but dressing up these mundane things by claiming that they are done for the good of the country is a lie. That was more or less my reply.

In point of fact, if the country were in danger, no one would be indifferent to the situation, no one! When the country is strong and there is no risk of war, when there is little chance of being attacked, nationalist ideas must retreat and individualism must fill the vacuum. We really must recognize this as reasonable. Contemporary Japan is not so secure, is it? It is a poor tiny country. As a result, anything can happen at any time. In light of this reality, we must all think about the country. However, Japan today is not a country that is about to collapse. Nor is it at all threatened by annihilation. Therefore, it is not necessary for us all to go around making a noise about it and chanting "The country, the country!" This is like running about town in fireproof clothing and being uncomfortable when there is no fire. When all is said and done, it is a matter of degree. If war comes or if the country falls into crisis, people whose mental faculties allow them to think, those who have created for themselves, through education and culture, a personality that obliges them to think, naturally direct their attention to the national situation. Then they put all their efforts into working for the good of the country, if necessary restricting their individual freedom and reducing their personal activities. We see here no more than the simple operation of natural laws. This is why I firmly believe that the two ideologies are not in any way involved in a conflictory process, in which they would contradict each other and engage in mortal combat. I would have liked to go into this topic more deeply, but as there is not enough time I will stop here.

There is only one other point that I would like to draw to your attention. When we compare the morality that espouses nationalism to that which professes individualism, the first seems to occupy a less important position. By their nature, countries, while appearing to be very fastidious as regards courtesy, do not show the same concerns in relation to morality. They engage in devious maneuvers, are hypocritical and cheating. Great confusion results from this behavior. When we take the country as a basis of assessment and envisage it as a monolithic entity, we must be calm and content ourselves with a low level of morality. On the other hand, if we take the perspective of individualism, then the importance of morality increases considerably. We must think about this difference. It seems obvious to me that in times of national peace and security, we must attach great importance to individualism and the high moral sense that arises from it. As I have run out of time, I must stop talking about this.

Today, I have come at your very kind invitation and I have made an effort to explain to you the need for individualism for you, gentlemen—you who will have the opportunity to live a fulfilling life on the personal level. I hope you will be able to use these suggestions as as a guide when you go out to play your part in the world. I cannot tell whether I have been able to make you understand. If the meaning of any of my points remains obscure for you, it is because I have not explained them sufficiently or properly. If anything seems ambiguous to you in what I have said, do not guess at my meaning but come and see me at my house, I beg you. I will do my best to give you an explanation whenever it is convenient for you. Even if you do not want to take so much trouble, nothing would give me greater pleasure than to know that you have understood the true meaning of my words. This lecture has lasted too long. I will now leave you in peace.

The Philosophical Foundations
of Literature

I had been asked to give a lecture at the opening session of the Congress of the Tokyo Fine Arts School Literature Society.[1] As I was employed by the *Asahi* newspaper, I was obliged to publish my personal convictions in it, and so, in spite of the inconvenience that it would cause him, I asked the Congress chairman to arrange for the shorthand version of my lecture to be sent to me. He graciously agreed to do this, and within three, four or five days I received the document accompanied by a short and very polite note. I do not know whether it was the inadequacy of my presentation or my inappropriate way of expressing myself, but on seeing these papers I realized that publishing my lecture in this form or anything like it would confuse the reader so much that it would addle his brain. So, I was forced to rewrite my text completely. When I began to tackle the task and laid out the shorthand documents in front of me, I realized that changes would have to be made everywhere and that the manuscript would end up almost double its original length.

In view of the nature of the subject, I deplore the fact that the obscurity of certain passages is sometimes attributable to a lack of connection between ideas, or to the tendency of the

---

[1] The lecture was given on April 20th, 1907, and the text that derived from it was published in the Tokyo *Asahi* newspaper between May 4th and June 4th of the same year.

argument to get lost in twists and turns so that it does not sustain the interest that it should naturally arouse. But obviously publication in a newspaper imposes certain constraints, and I have therefore to accept the disadvantages and divide the lecture into daily installments of one or two columns.

As far as the long story that you will find below is concerned, other than having to work from the shorthand transcription of the lecture, there are no disadvantages, I think, in having produced an essay written for a newspaper from it. I will omit from this article the "Draft Introduction"[2] which I wrote as a member of the *Asahi Shimbun* production team and in which I introduced myself to my readers. I am convinced that, by airing my convictions regarding Art and Literature, I do my duty to my public, which consists in clearly giving my point of view and indicating my aspirations.

1. Introduction

I have not given many lectures. In fact, the expression "not many" is inaccurate: I have given hardly any. I have often been invited to give lectures but, until today, have always declined the invitation. I find the task really unpleasant, you know. Besides, I am not skilled enough. When it comes to teaching lessons, on the other hand, I do that on a daily basis, so it seems to me that I should have some ability in that respect. However, as you have unfortunately asked me to give you a lecture, it has to be assumed that something insipid and clumsy will come out of it.

In fact, Mr Ōmura[3] came to see me and asked me to give a lecture on any subject I chose. Since it was unfortunate for him

---

[2] "Nyū-sha-no-ji," published in the Tokyo *Asahi Shimbun* on May 3rd, 1907. In this document, the writer explains the circumstances that brought him to occupy his new duties.

[3] Ōmura Seigai (1868–1927), a professor of history of Western and Eastern Art in the Tokyo Fine Arts School.

that he had decided to give me the responsibility of this lecture even though he was aware of my clumsiness in such matters, I tried to get him to give up the idea. He would not agree at all, and pressed me strongly to do it, urging, "Give this lecture at all costs! Any subject will do. Please give it."

I punctuated his speech with shakes of my head. In the end, he said to me, "You do not have to give a lecture!"

"If I don't give a lecture, what must I do then?" I asked him.

"Well, be there, show your face to everyone; they will understand you. That will be enough."

Those were his gracious words. At that point I, too, made a great decision, and telling myself I had nothing to fear in such circumstances, I readily accepted his offer. That is why I am here before you today. But, unfortunately, my face should not be shown to anyone. As I think that the face alone is not at all important, what if we pass on to something else? It goes without saying, gentlemen, that it will be quite impossible to call this a lecture. And even if we were talking about a lecture, it would seem in reality more like a sermon. When I give a lesson, my principle is not to recite something from memory but to talk in the classroom, forcing myself to write down everything I say. Today, I do not have time for that; nor have I assembled the necessary ideas. Therefore, a lecture that should have been good will be bad, only for today, against all expectations.

I find it extremely interesting that you organize a congress on literature in a School of Fine Arts and that, apart from artistry and technique, knowledge and taste in literature develop on a general level. As the Headmaster, Mr Masaki,[4] has just said, we can establish very strong relationships between literature and the arts and so, given that you represent art and that you also have a certain interest in literature, in submitting for

---

[4] Masaki Naohiko (1862–1940). He was the headmaster of the Tokyo Fine Arts School from 1902 to 1931.

your information a clumsy rendering such as mine, and in view of the contacts that exist between the two parties—artists and men of letters—I consider myself very honored to have been afforded this opportunity to give you my humble opinion. I told you just now that I had promised something very unusual, since I know better than to attempt a lecture which, for the reasons I have given you, I am not sufficiently skilled to do. I beg you please not to show the least gratitude to me in any way. I came here considering it a very great honor. I repeat that I am not skilled enough to give a lecture and that it is also impossible for me to assemble my ideas in the form of a lesson. It has to be assumed that the result will be something that will sound bad and will offend your ears; and I ask your forgiveness in advance.

I am going to start the job slowly and begin my lecture. When I anticipate that I am going to start in a particular manner, this may sound promising, but in truth there is nothing in it. I have before my eyes three or four pages in a notebook, and from this point on the substance of what I am going to say to you will be limited to these three or four pages. It should go very smoothly and, after a quarter of an hour, I should have finished. But for a lecture that is given *en passant*, it is fairly poor. So, starting from these three or four pages and talking wildly, I am going to go on developing my ideas. I have not thought in advance how to develop them. I do not know in what part of my lecture and in what direction I shall carry out these developments. From time to time, I will make unforeseen detours. I will not stop where I ought to stop. At points where I ought to go back, I will probably not go back. This is the very sad method of developing my ideas that I shall use. But even though I do not know whether this is really the beginning, I am perhaps going to start and you must not be at all surprised. I should like you to listen to me quietly because, sooner or later, slipping and stumbling, I will manage to steer myself in the deep direction of the relationship between art and literature. In the speech that

Mr Masaki has just given, he used the expression "the charac-teristic state of mind of tradesmen and craftsmen." I myself will use the vague and little used idea of "starting point." But if you wish to know the direction that I shall take, taking the bit between my teeth, well, I intend, like the headmaster to consid-er the characteristic state of mind of tradesmen and craftsmen.

2. Relationships between the Ego and the Outside World

In the first place, I am standing here and you are all sitting down there. I am standing on this low platform while you are sitting in a raised position. So, in reality, I am sitting and you are stand-ing. If I express what I call "reality" by using another word, I can be designated by the term "Ego" and you, in relation to me, are the "non-Ego." To put it in a more complicated way, this reali-ty is the opposition between the Ego and the outside world. In other words, the world is comprised of reciprocal reactions between the Ego and the "outside." I assume that you all per-ceive this in the same way as I do—everyone has this reaction. Therefore, when I give my lecture I am here and you are there; there is between us what we call "distance." This distance will be two meters, four meters, even twenty or forty. Is this room so big? I don't know. But, in any case, whatever the size of this room, expressed in tsubos, I am standing here and you are sit-ting down over there. We call this expanse "space." Even if you do not call it that, you are very familiar with it: in short, there is what we call "space." All the objects in this room occupy a particular place. Today, the conference started at 1 o'clock in the afternoon. We don't know when it will finish, but it will finish at one time or another. I think that it should end before night-fall. In carrying out this task, I will tell stories which do not have beginnings or ends. Then, when I have finished, Mr Ueda[5] will

---

[5] Ueda Bin (1874–1916), a specialist in English literature and a poet. At this time, he was teaching English literature at the Tokyo Imperial University.

replace me and you will again have an interesting conference. After that, the session will be closed. Mr Ueda's address and my own are events that experience development. And if this development, which we identify as "time," did not exist, nothing would happen. This is also true for everyone and there is no need for us to go over it again. Finally, if you ask me why I came here to give a lecture and talk on and on, and if you think I am here because of a moment of madness or some sort of whim, well, I would hesitate a little before replying. There is a reciprocal affinity here. In other words, different affinities have come together as, for example, the polite request which Mr Tamura made to me, my slight commitment, the sense of duty that motivated me once I had given him my word. The result was that I put on my overcoat and came here. These relationships, which deal with questions touching people and nature, are called "causality laws."

So, that's the way it goes. I, a being, live in this world. There are other people, who are you. We are all in the middle of this vast space, where we act out our play. This play develops as time passes. This development is conceptualized as subject to "causality laws." It follows that in this place, we must first recognize that I exist, then the fact that you exist, in what are called space and time. Similarly, as there are "causality laws," we must recognize that they govern us. This seems indisputable and it is what I think myself.

However, if we consider this proposition seriously, it is very debatable. Certainly, everyone normally thinks that way—I do myself. But if we stand back a little and distance ourselves from

---

Subsequently, he became a professor at the Kyoto Imperial University. His collection of translations of poetry, *The Sound of the Tide* (*Kai cho on*), published in 1905, greatly influenced the Japanese poetry world. On the day of the conference, April 20th, 1907, he gave a lecture on the English critic Walter Horatio Pater, as the writer Shiga Naoya mentions in his *Diary*.

an incidental way of thinking, it is very odd. I have the impression that things are not as I have described. For some reason, this "I" whom I mentioned at the beginning, who put on a coat, has put on a stiff collar and has let his moustache grow, seems to exist beyond doubt. But the true nature of this "I" is eminently suspect. It is clear that this coat and this stiff collar can be touched, but they are not "I." If I were asked whether this body whose hand or foot I scratch when it itches or which I stroke when it hurts, is really "I," well I would respond that no, it is no one. What we call "itching" or "pain" are sensations. Scratching or stroking oneself is a response to a psychological desire. However, apart from this, there is nothing that is hand or foot. By convention, this phenomenon of which we are aware and which we call hand or foot is precisely the phenomenon that makes one hurt or itch. In short, it is awareness. And rather than saying "to be aware," which implies a state, a more active rendering would be more appropriate. It is only that which seems perfectly to express my thoughts. Anyway, I am unable to prove what I describe, but it is a fact that we cannot oppose and it is clear that, in this case, proof is not indispensable. When we examine this question more closely, we see that what is commonly called "I" is not something that exists in this world on an objective level but something that results from a continuity of awareness which we call "I" for convenience. Why do we make waves in a calm sea? Why do we wonder whether it is practical to create a superfluous being (subject) which is called "I"? Why do we create this "I" and, in contrast, a being which is not I but you? It is this phenomenon that causes the differentiation between the "I" and the outside world.

3. The Phenomenon of Awareness

In saying this, not only do I deny the Self (or what we ordinarily call the Self); the statement also negates your existence. Therefore, however large you are in number, I feel very, very sorry for you, because in spite of appearances it is as if you were dead. Perhaps you will be angry; however, since it is a question of bringing the discussion down to essentials, I would ask you first to listen to my point of view. Since I talk about essentials, I am hardly being cavalier, but you who are distant from me exist only on the objective level. I have said that you are distant from me and, since this Ego does not exist as far as I am concerned, a *fortiori*, as far as you are concerned it is even more true that you do not exist. However much we may fear this, there is nothing to be done about it. You are over there. When you think you are there, you are there. I, too, think something similar. When I say you are there, you are there—but this is possible only if you think it. This means that however much further one might wish to take this notion, as we do not even have proof of what I have just suggested, we cannot do anything. Normally, to prove that something exists we look at it, do we not? Basing our perception on what we have seen, we try to touch it with our hands. Then we try to sniff it or taste it. Perhaps it is not necessary to take so much trouble to prove your existence. However, as I said before, with our eyes we try to see, with our ears we try to hear, but at the fundamental level it is a question only of becoming aware of the senses of sight and hearing and, if this process of being aware is changed, there is no reason for objects and beings independent from us to exist. When I see or touch you, it is only awareness operating in me which makes the shadows clothed in black students' uniforms with gold buttons appear, because nothing else allows my perception or recognition of the reality of your existence. Therefore, having maturely reflected on the subject, we could say that I myself do not exist and neither do you. Other than that, there is really nothing but awareness. If the gold buttons are reflected in my eyes, it is because I am becoming aware of the gold buttons. If the ceiling of this conference hall is darkening, it is only because we are becoming aware that these places are becoming darker. Don't think that I am being scornful when I suggest these things to you. Given that it is impossible to say that the ceiling of the Fine Arts School is dirty, but that it is simply a question of being aware of blackness, there is no slander—since I do not admit the existence of an objective world this, I think, has no importance.

That is all I wanted to say to begin. When we stand back from banal reflections and find ourselves in a universe sustained by relationships between the "I" and the outside world, it is impossible to talk about a situation in which the outside world can demonstrate its existence independently and it is also impossible for me to say that I live separately from the outside world. To put this another way, the outside world separate from the "I" no longer exists; and it therefore follows unsurprisingly that the "I" does not exist independently of the outside world. The phrase "relationships between the 'I' and the outside world" originates in the need to establish an exact correspondence with this situation. We use the two characters "Butsu" (the outside world) and "Ga" (the "I") only to facilitate understanding. But at a fundamental level, there is really no way of separating the two and, given this impossibility, terms such as "exact correspondence" become redundant. The conclusion, then, is that the only thing that clearly exists is awareness. And what I call the "continuity of awareness" is, in plain words, what we call life.

As I use the character for "continuity" (Renzoku), I include the implication that awareness undergoes changes and develops, and, given this process of development, (1) awareness must comprise several elements, (2) these elements must experience ups and downs, (3) insofar as the ups and downs emerge, the awareness of these elements must be clear, and (4) as the development of awareness is subject to a certain extent to rules, the question becomes singularly complicated. But today is not the appropriate time to talk to you about this boring subject; and as it is an area for which I rely entirely on your research, I will go on to the rest of my lecture. In any case, as far as the principles of awareness development are concerned, which comprise the four points I have just mentioned, I have expressed my own ideas, despite their many imperfections, in the fifth part of "Upon Literature," and so I take the liberty of referring you to that work. I take this opportunity to recommend that you each order a volume of "Upon Literature." So, anyway, it is a question of awareness. There are no external objects—and nor, most probably, is there "I." Awareness is the only thing of which we can be certain. And this is proof of continuity. Whether we try to explain this continuity of awareness from a philosophical point of view or in the sense of development, it undoubtedly occurs. I will, therefore, proceed by taking this into account.

4. The Continuity of Awareness

If I pause for a moment and consider what I said at the outset of my lecture, it now seems to me to be a little strange. I mentioned right at the beginning that there was a being called the "I." I said that you were certainly present and that, reciprocally, we were getting into that dubious thing called "space," and that we were punting forward, on an unknown current called "time," being hindered by something frightening called "causality laws," and that we were suffering because of this. When we reflect on these matters by placing ourselves above everyday events, it seems that the complete opposite is the case. The relationship between the "I" and the outside world, for example, has never existed. The universe that is "I" has, consequently, become something very important. I do not know whether this view derives from a sudden change of mind, but it is completely contradictory. (Space, time and causality laws are, of course, a part of this great upheaval. As I have said all this in continuation of today's lecture, it will become clearer as the lecture progresses.)

Why do such contradictions occur? It is as well to ask this question: in spite of my statement that there is nothing, however much we try to eradicate everything on the ordinary level that comprises the universe, such eradication proves impossible and the cosmos satisfies us. Thus I want to say that, even though I am not Mr Tobari,[6] speaking as if I were him, the world is in front of me and I, Tobari Chikufū, am here. Why do such contradictions appear? That is really a great problem. If we were to debate it in a complex way using difficult language, I think it would take a long time. Taking account of practical necessities, I must speak on a subject simplified to the extreme in a very short period of time. It goes without saying that, if distinguished philosophers or people of similar rank were to hear me, they would burst out, I think, with violent criticisms, saying that my thoughts were unfinished. However, in the short time I have been allowed, I can rid myself of this subject, which has been exaggerated. Naturally, it cannot be said that I have achieved perfection. It is imperfect, of course. Please praise me, telling me that such courage on my part is admirable. Of course, regardless of the time allowed, if I were asked to formulate this argument in more elegant terms, my performance would perhaps not be convincing. Well, that is just what is required.

Why do such contradictions occur? If we could supply a one-word answer, there would be no problem. As I have already said, our lives—the word "our" is an inappropriate term because it creates a relationship between the "I" and others, but I will use it for reasons of convenience—our lives are a continuity of awareness. And we have no wish to disrupt this continuity in any way: in other words, we do not want to die. If I could use yet another expression, I would say that the fact that this continuity persists pleases us infinitely. I cannot explain to you why it pleases us. No one coming on to this platform could explain

---

[6] Tobari Chikufū (1873–1955) who, under his real name Shinichirō, was a specialist in German literature and a critic. He introduced Nietzsche to Japanese readers with his publications in the magazine *Teikoku bungaku*.

it. However, we cannot but recognize it as true: that is indisputable. Of course, if we brought in an expert on the subject from the evolutionist school, he might show us some kind of natural order in the progression of this phenomenon by explaining that this desire to stay alive derives from the development of habit over a long period. This would mean that those who were deprived of this drive, who did not conform to the demands of the world, would inevitably die. It would therefore also be possible to support the hypothesis that those who are alive today are only misers clinging on to life. Further, there is no doubt why this band of irresolute, dirty beings, extremely attached to life, are full of energy. All these suggestions may provide some explanation for the phenomenon, but when we advance further into the logic, and try to complete the investigation and discover the principal cause for this tendency, we are defeated. And we reach a situation in which we should take something that would be close to art from the Zen paradox that says that we will go back to where all laws have their source, where we will go into a place which is the Entire, the Uniform, the unmixed Pure. Schopenhauer himself describes the tendency as the "blind will to live"[7] and this is truly a very useful expression. I thought about borrowing it for a few moments. But, if I wished to build on any concept like that, which is very strange, outside the continuity of awareness, I would have to beg your forgiveness for the commitment I made just now when I said there was nothing apart from the continuity of awareness. But I am going to stop talking about this subject, even though that is a pity. We must consider this tendency as forming part of

---

[7] "Blinder Wille zum Leben." This idea is developed by Arthur Schopenhauer (Dantzig, 1788; Frankfurt-am-Main, 1860), a German philosopher, in particular in his principal work, *The World as Will and Representation* (1818), where he expounded a philosophy of will. Limitless and purposeless "will to live" is absurd and is characterized by suffering and boredom.

the continuity of awareness, and, therefore, its attribute. And the concept I call "this tendency" is recognized as having emerged as such after considerable development, and is the result of a process of abstraction. Whatever the case, the fact that we are unquestionably searching for this continuity is the only thing we can accept as real. To clarify, I state with certitude that there is in awareness a tendency to continuity and that this is a reality that I hold to be true.

5. The Content of Awareness

When we talk about awareness, of continuity, of the tendency to continuity, we naturally include the idea of division and unification. If continuity does not exist, if we have no awareness of the fact that A follows B, the two awarenesses which allow us to distinguish between A and B cannot be clearly developed. The fact of talking about differentiation is equivalent to saying that it is possible, simultaneously, to unify the same or similar awarenesses. To provide an example, when the awareness that we call the "sense of sight" is differentiated from other senses, such as the senses of touch and taste, a global unification of the awareness of vision occurs and thus the term "sense of sight," which expresses it, becomes possible. First, this process of differentiation must take place and then, by relating the differentiated awareness of vision with the organ we call the eyeball, we may well become aware that this type of awareness is governed by the eyeball. Let us imagine that the awareness of sight is combined with the function of the eyeball: until this process of differentiation has occurred, sight will not necessarily be identified with the eyeball. Perhaps, if I had lived a long time ago, I would have looked at an object with my whole body, maybe licking it in the process. The division of tasks between the eyes, ears, nose and tongue is, I think, a recent occurrence. And when this division appears, the phenomenon of accommodation no longer operates. If you contract tongue cancer, you do not eat with your heel. If you suffer from gonorrhea, you cannot urinate through your navel. These are extremely impractical examples, but as soon as you talk about the continuity of awareness, as soon as the meaning of this term "continuity" becomes clear, there is no doubt that the content of the awareness which forms this continuity must also be clear. It is impossible to know for certain whether an awareness which was not clear would become continuous. This would be contrary to our fundamental tendency. Or rather, it goes against what we call "awareness." The division and unification of awareness develop naturally from that fundamental tendency. In future, how far will these processes of division and unification go? It is practically impossible to imagine. But we do not know, in relation to that question, to what extent the senses complicate matters. The things that we cannot see today with the naked eye, that we cannot touch with our hands, or even those things that go beyond the five senses, are progressively, I think, entering into our field of awareness. And so, it seems to me, the best thing for us is to take our time and wait.

I repeat once again: I am talking about the "continuity of awareness." When we break down this expression, we obtain the character for "awareness" and that for "continuity." If we respond to this division into two parts by asking what is the content of the awareness and what sequence does the continuity follow, the general problem of awareness confronts us. Combining those questions, we have the following problem: how can we achieve a continuity of awareness with a certain content which follows a certain sequence? When we encounter this problem—we have already encountered it, it cannot be otherwise—there is behind it the dilemma of recognizing awareness as reality. And underlying that dilemma is the question of choice. If we do not have a certain freedom or margin of choice, we will find no solution to the problem. The answer lies in the possibility of finding several methods of resolution.

The principle of assessment, which is the problem to be resolved, is based on what we call the "ideal." If I put all this together into one statement, I would say that we have a tendency to want to live. Perhaps the proposition that there is a tendency to continuity in awareness will not be disputed. Through this tendency, choice is expressed and the choice originates in the ideal. And so, up to now, a tendency to say that it is sufficient to live has developed; today we are beginning to attribute a particular meaning to this desire for life. Thus, whether we achieve continuity of awareness following a certain sequence or choose a particular content of awareness, the ideal is broken down into these two orientations and develops gradually. Later, the ideal of the man of letters who talks to you will be explained.

If we once again examine the meaning of the characters making up the word "awareness," according to this process of reciprocal differentiation where there is continuity, the awareness must be absolutely clear. And, therefore, according to the degree of differentiation that occurs, when we see the awareness undergoing a sort of metabolism, there must be a sequence according to which A disappears and B makes its appearance. Since, according to this sequence, the awareness of B occurs after the departure of A, when we become aware of B, A is no longer in our field of awareness. In spite of this, the differentiation between A and B can operate: as the origin of the awareness of B is clear, it must be assumed that an awareness of A exists, even if it is comparatively blurred. Commonly we call this blurred awareness "memory." This is why memory is at its most intense at high levels of awareness (that is, when the clarity of awareness is greatest) and at its weakest when embedded in the lowest layers of awareness.

6. Time, Space, Numbers and Causality Relationships (1)

Thus, continuity of awareness cannot be understood without memory, and any discussion about memory inevitably entails the notion of time. This leads to the proposition that what we call "time" describes our experience of waiting for a continuity of awareness. "Time" perceived independently, with no relationship to this process of waiting for a continuity of awareness, could not exist in this world. In other words, it could be said that there is some sort of relationship between awareness and the duration of awareness and that, as long as there is awareness, this phenomenon will occur. Thus, moving away from awareness and considering this type of relationship independently should present no difficulty on the level of abstraction, if we wish to consider abstraction for the sake of it. But I cannot say that it exists for me. It is exactly as if one were to point to the white color inside this water jug in front of me and stubbornly insist that the white color existed separately from the material substance. If we reflect on this a little, what we call "time" passes and, within this continuum, events seem to develop and evolve. But this has no other meaning than to allow, for convenience, existence in the form of an abstraction of what we call "time" as a result of the progression up to now of those forces of differentiation and unification that I mentioned earlier. I think the logic is similar to arguing that, in extracting the scent of a rose, the rose is in the scent. My reflections lead me to think that, rather than saying that the rose is in the scent, it would be more appropriate to say that the scent is in the rose. However, identifying what we call "time" or even "space," which I shall mention soon, is a very difficult problem, and a philosopher would say that it is an extremely annoying subject. As a result, when someone like myself expresses at random the probability of normal ideas, it would perhaps be better for you not to be too trustful. However, it would be appropriate to give some credence to it—I think that would be preferable. Until the end of this lecture, you will believe in it. Then, when you get home, I think it will be quite all right for you not to believe in it any more.

Next, let us look further at this continuity of awareness that I am talking about. It happens that A goes out and B comes in. First, we are aware of A, then of B. This time, we will reverse the order: after becoming aware of B, we go back to A. And whether we extend or shorten the period over which we become aware of the two, the relationship between the two occasions of becoming aware does not change. Then, we become aware that this relationship is relatively independent and that it is, moreover, a definite relationship. At the same time, we understand that it is impossible for us to return to relationships in time and that we express this through the expression "spatial relationship." Thus, this also seems to be a relationship that exists between the two awarenesses and, considered independently of such awareness, what constitutes space cannot exist. The very fact that the concept of space has developed reveals the existence of this abstraction and is the result of taking into consideration the reality of its existence. It cannot be otherwise. As far as grammar is concerned, this is something that consists of gathering together reciprocal relationships in the form of rules that have as their object the arrangement of language. But the man in the street has grammar within him, and so he thinks in the form of sentences. And in the same way that grammar, comprising words and sentences, is not limited to demonstrating the relationships between words—as grammar is clearly intimately connected to sentences—it can equally be said, in my opinion, that the concept of space also comprises within itself this double awareness that is achieved through practical application. For reasons of convenience, we have made it seem remote by abstracting it, and when we have progressively evacuated this large space for outside, we will have experienced an impression similar to that which we experience when faced with things that are scattered in all directions. However, as there is some difficulty in commenting on this space on a theoretical level, it is worth remembering that Newton affirmed the existence of space on an objective level, that Kant himself talked about "intuition," and that therefore, as regards the subject on which I am speaking, do not trust anything I say. If you do trust my suggestions, this does not lend itself to argument and I do not think there is any difficulty. But, even if I am the only one to think so, the fact that I am dealing with this subject at all is a consequence of the fact that I have been asked to give you a lecture and that I must do so at all costs. And if I do not talk to you about this, however long I remain standing on this platform, it will be impossible for me to pass on to a literary subject.

In attributing an objective existence to space and time, we have invented what we call numbers as a convenient means of measuring these abstract concepts so that we can make use of them. These silly things that we call numbers have no real existence—well, there is no proof that they existed in the past any more than in the present. As far as numbers are concerned, I think that it is extremely difficult to conceptualize these signs, whose only function is the measurement, in the simplest way, of relationships of continuity, without reference to the content of awareness.

7. Time, Space, Numbers and Causality Relationships (2)

Thus, within the continuity of awareness, it follows that the number 2 or a number larger than 2 is always connected in the same order. After A, B must appear. It always appears. No change affects the order. As regards this particular form of relationship, not only do we give it the name of "causality," but also, simply by seeing such relationships in isolation, we fabricate what we call laws of causality. This expression "fabricate" may seem odd, but we are talking about making something appear that has no real appearance, and so we can proceed in no other way than by fabricating it. A causality that is not accompanied by the phenomenon of awareness is an empty causality. The "laws of causality," in other words, is in itself a phrase without substance and we use it purely for convenience. Not knowing this, and ending definitively with a statement like "we are governed by the fundamental laws of the universe" would be equivalent to trembling at a paper tiger! What we call the laws of causality have been limited up to now to serving as an index to show at a glance that something has actually occurred. This is practical, but in future a thought such as "the continuity of awareness that would have transcended these laws of causality cannot occur" would be the height of stupidity. Because of this, people who have properly understood will find nothing strange in the fact that ordinary people are strange. The reason for this is that, apart from the causalities identified so far, they know that an endless number of causality relationships are possible. This is little different from the fact that when the bell rings people think without fail that lunchtime has arrived.

Now, if we summarize the points that I have made so far, I think we could progress from the starting point to a more advanced place. (1) We are totally dominated by what we can call a thirst for life, and at the level of awareness, a tendency to continuity takes shape. (2) This tendency to continuity gives to free choice. (3) The choice gives to the ideal. (4) As a result, awareness, realizing this ideal, has a tendency to continuity that becomes particular, or specific. (5) The result of this is that awareness is divided (broken up), gains in clarity and unifies. (6) By unifying in the form of determined relationships, awareness attributes an objective existence to time. (7) By unifying in the form of determined relationships, awareness attributes an objective existence to space. (8) So that the concepts of time and space can be used, awareness fabricates an abstract entity for the purpose, and hence we have numbers. (9) In unifying this continuity over time, awareness produces the notion of causality and is abstracted in the form of the laws of causality.

This is what, roughly speaking, occurs first. When we examine them more closely, what we call space, what we call time, what we call the laws of causality are nothing but hypotheses, used for convenience. In reality, these things do not exist. It is I who say this. If you do not say the same thing, it is not important—that will do. It is up to you! Anyway, it seems to me that, just for today, I want to take this as a hypothesis. If I do not proceed in this way, my lecture cannot progress. If we wonder why we remain impassive about the adoption of such a useless hypothesis, well, this is because we are moved by human sentiments and we only think about wishing to live. Wishing to live! In pursuing this objective, we accomplish normal tasks without worrying at all about whether they are based on lies or errors. We think that space must exist and that, if it does not, daily life will not be so convenient and so we immediately invent space in all its aspects. If time does not exist, we feel that is a tiresome thing. All right, let it be so! Let us create time. Then here is time immediately created. In this way, through different abstractions and various hypotheses, with which we are all concerned, when anything is too painful we prefer the lesser of two evils—and a lie that allows us to settle the problem makes its appearance. Then truth has come out of this lie. Perhaps this is because this lie is very convenient or because, in this present age of decadence, we have learnt to fabricate the lie over many years. I myself took this to be true and you have taken the same approach. We do not see anything wrong in it, or anything to cause doubt or give rise to the slightest hesitation. We have taken this hypothesis for reality, and indeed we are very happy to accept it. We say that the state of poverty leads to stupidity, and that being at the end of our resources causes excesses of behavior. We, too, when we are beset by the difficulties of life, descend to a similar level. In short, because of the demands of everyday life, we have invented this lie by a process of deduction—and so the truth is included in it in the same way as there is truth in the situation of the prostitute who weeps on St Sylvester's day. You will ask me why. Well, here it is: if time did not exist, and if the numbers that allow us to measure time did not exist either, although I committed myself to giving this lecture on a Saturday, perhaps I would have come and given it on a Sunday; and then there would have been problems for some of us. If we did not have the notion of space, we could not go out of the door of the tram, it would be impossible to get down from the first floor, we would always be at the police station, and we would tread on the dog's tail. This would not be a very agreeable situation. And it is the same for laws of causality that pervade normal life. If we did not grant the right of existence to all these concepts, we would be dangerous people. We must do so in order not to be danger-ous, even at the price of foolish actions. People who strut around and display their spirit of excess are irremediably wedded to death. As a result, and as I am sure you know, humanity today is healthy and is composed only of pedants and dishonest men, and that those who belonged to a virtuous past have been hit by the tram, have fallen into the river or have been arrested by the police and are all dead, without exception.

8. The Opposition between the Ego and the Outside World: The Process of Differentiation Carried Out by Awareness (1)

If the existence of space and time is possible, it should be easy to separate awareness into two parts, the Ego and the outside world. No uproar will be caused by the contention that it is easy. In reality, after separating the Ego from outside objects to locate it skillfully in place, it is exactly as if we had constructed the cen-tral building of a temple to shelter space and time. Whether we are ready or not for this central building to be created, we take hold of awareness and throw it in someone else's face. We take hold of it; then we throw it back. We throw it in someone else's face with an energy like that of a maker of birdseed cake who breaks up the mixture and throws it with all his strength into the soya flour. If we consider that the soya flour is time, this becomes a cake in the past, present or even in the future. If we consider this soya flour as representing space, then we obtain a faraway cake, a nearby cake, a cake that is here or even a cake that is over there. At present, about 150 of you are assembled in order in front of me. Please forgive my inaccuracies about you, but it is I who for convenience have thrown you here. As space exists today, even if it is a lie, and given that we possess treasures which we do not use, well, space is there, and I project you into it making the same noise as if you were birdseed cakes, you who number over a hundred people assembled here in perfect alignment. This is really convenient. When I said I had thrown you into this space, I was impertinent; but as I do not take you for millet cakes, I think you need not be put out about it.

By connecting this process of radiation with the process of division I have described, not defining anything which is other than ourselves simply as an object or a being that is outside us, but giving this phenomenon various names, we make in effect a reciprocal distinction. For example, I would make a distinction between a perceptible object and a supra-perceptible object (that is, something whose true form we do not know, such as a god or ghost, and of whose existence we cannot be certain). What I understand by perceptible objects can be distinguished by, among other things, taste which we experience with our tongue, smell which we sniff with our nose, sound or resonance which we can detect with our ears, or forms or colors which we see with our eyes. And similarly, we will proceed to distinguish much more precisely the items that we have classified in this basic way. If we proceed by differentiation, as perception becomes more refined, classification becomes more and more subtle. Thus there is not only an initial transformation into plants, trees, animals or humans, but a further refinement so that plants metamorphose into violets, dandelions or primroses. Trees appear in the form of plum trees, peach trees, pines or Japanese cypresses. Animals will be cows, horses, monkeys or dogs. Humans are divided into soldiers, peasants, craftsmen, tradesmen or people of the Third Age, young people, men, women or nobles, humble people, chiefs, submissive people, wise people, stupid people, just and corrupt people. And all these refinements divide and branch out as much as we want them to. Today, the varieties of flowers and plants that botanists are able to distinguish are, I think, nearly a hundred times more numerous than human categories. Would it then be incomprehensible to suggest that artists such as you, gentlemen, could distinguish about ten times more colors than ordinary people? If we ask why this phenomenon occurs, if our reflections take us back to the source of our suggestions, in short we find ourselves compelled to undertake this process of differentiation in order to satisfy our burning desire to live. It is for no other purpose than to enlarge our field of awareness in advance so that our continuity of awareness can be exercised freely to provide a sufficient margin for us to carve out an area of choice. However much we look at a plant, we can all only see uniformly the color green. However much we may want to be aware of all the different varieties of green, given that the phenomenon of differentiation does not go so far, however hard we try, our effort will be in vain. At least as far as colors are concerned, complex daily life, full of changes, ends in something that is impossible to explain. In fact, the cloak of blindness has been thrown over it. This is regrettable in my opinion. In the words of a critic, where we see only one color Titian[8] sees fifty. The practical aspect of this does not derive solely from the fact

---

[8] Titiano Vecellio, better known as Titian (Pieve di Cadore, about 1490—Venice, 1576), an Italian painter. He left his native town for Venice where he worked with the Bellinis, then with Giorgione. *Bacchus and Ariadne* (1523, National Gallery)

that Titian was an artist. I mean to say that a person's daily life accommodates itself to circumstances in a relative manner. As the items making up awareness become more numerous, freedom of choice is expanded. This continuity of awareness can easily be accomplished and as a result a situation is produced in which the individual's ideal can easily be realized. And, to speak of man, what I shall call by the name of man has a faculty of accommodation. It is not simply a question of colors. For example, consider the life that poor people lead ideally. We are like color. This is something wretched and worthy of compassion. Even if we are not irked by money problems, even if we are the issue of a noble and illustrious lineage, the continuity of awareness, with uniformity and banality, causes us to lead a life which is very like that of an amoeba, as if we have been plunged into shadow or mist, without there being the slightest ideal and without there being the slightest difference between high and low, refinement or vulgarity, justice and injustice, duplicity and honesty. As far as ordinary people are concerned, we react as if human beings were identical objects. And if we draw attention to this by arguing that it is a result of our ignoring our intelligence, this creates more difficulties, because people mistrust us and mock us. But this is not a subject for discussion here. The lecture has deviated from its main subject and has fallen into the very center of a muddy ditch. Let us quickly return and continue our progress in a straight line!

9. The Process of Differentiation Carried Out by Awareness (2)

As I have just said, we locate objects in space by radiation and carry out a meticulous classification of them by processes of differentiation. At the same time, we develop for ourselves a process similar to differentiation that leads to separation between body and mind. We divide this operation of the mind into three: intelligence, perception and will. Then, dividing up

intelligence and perception, by the specificity of these operations we can proceed to make various distinctions. As people
who we call psychologists are mainly responsible for this area of
choice, it is very easy to listen to their pronouncements.
However, abusive practices slip into the work of psychologists
during analysis in which recommendations are made that proceed from the heart/mind and from the resulting process of
abstraction. Perhaps intelligence, perception and will derive
from a purposely established classification, but these faculties are
not isolated from one another and cannot be exercised in the
absence of a relationship with the outside world. As regards
operations that proceed from the heart/mind, however much
they intervene, however subtle the elements, we can truly say,
when we consider them as a whole, that there are many cases in
which these three faculties, intelligence, perception and will, are
united. Therefore, the fact of carrying out a clear-cut classification into these three distinct faculties is an abstraction to which
we yield only for convenience. If we have no recourse to these
procedures of abstraction, the task of transcribing the movements of the heart/mind as a whole, which become extremely
subtle as the process of differentiation is taken to a critical point,
so that they can be revealed to people, falls principally on men
of letters. Thus, the work of these people allows us to progress
towards a clear state of awareness of something that had been
plunged in obscurity and to carry out a meticulous breakdown
and classification of that of which we have become aware. For
example, in the works of the past such as *The Bamboo Cutter's
Story*[9] or *The Chronicle of the Great Peace*,[10] the various characters

---

[9] *The Bamboo Cutter's Story* (*Taketori monogatari*) dating from the end of the
ninth or the beginning of the tenth century. This work seems to be the first
of the "popular stories" in prose.

[10] *The Chronicle of the Great Peace* (*Taiheiki*), an epic dating from the end of the
fourteenth century that tells in forty books the history of fifty years of war and
troubles (1318–67).

all resemble human beings. It is the same with Saikaku.[11] At the end of the day, the human race has been seen, mostly, by writers who, uttering cries of admiration, pain, disgust, joy or sadness, have probably proceeded with the same complete distraction. With the coming of the present age, in which operations of differentiation have developed, conceptions concerning humanity were no longer marked with nobility. As regards operations that proceed from the mind, if writers did not have the ability to divide things up in a fine and clear manner, and to describe minutely the parts thus divided, they would be out of step with the doctrines of the present time. When people who do not have this singular perspicacity try to represent other people, they behave exactly as if they have become color-blind and want to paint something, and nothing but complete failure can result. In your case, gentlemen, whose speciality is painting, if you did not have the visual skills to distinguish between the whiteness of a sheet of paper and the whiteness of a tablecloth, it would be impossible for you to render colors according to the ideal which you have made of them. It is the same with men of letters: when they are faced with individuals of the same temperament, the same orientations, from the same environment and of the same age, without the perceptive abilities to identify a fine differentiation between the individuals, they will be unable to describe adequately the human personality. As a result, for a man of letters who writes about people it is not enough just to be a professional man of letters; he must also be someone whose power of discernment with regard to people has developed to a high degree. In our ordinary world, which

---

[11] Ihara Saikaku (ca. 1642–93) was apparently a wealthy trader living in the town of Osaka, who had always been a poet. In 1673, he published his first collection of haiku (*Ten Thousand Haiku of Ikutama*). In 1675, he composed a thousand haiku in one day in memory of his wife, who died at the age of twenty-five.

continues to make progress, if we do not possess a highly developed sense of perception (this ability is not limited to men of letters—ordinary people can have great skill in this area), we will assuredly find our hands tied. In this mundane world, we do not think in this way. If we wonder what type of people novelists are, simply because they are novelists, we think that novelists earn their living simply by licking their pens, that it is a normal craft like that of the cabinetmaker or wallpaper hanger. We hold university professors in much more esteem than novelists. We also defer more to government ministers, rich people, aristocrats and so on. This is strange, if we wish to learn about the new reality of what we call human beings, because it is precisely novelists who can show us the differentiations among us. I think that it could be said that through the work of novelists, we are exhorted to progress little by little, and that they open up a road for us through thick scrub leading to development and civilization. I do not mean to say that the merit of a novelist is limited to this single point. However much I discuss this and consider it, novelists in one respect are like office managers or even government doctors. If you say, gentlemen, that there is not a single novelist in Japan today, I would respond that it is the fault of contemporary Japanese novelists (if you wish, you can consider me as one of them). Like office managers who are not worthy of the name, doctors who are not worthy of the title, well, we are in an identical situation and all we novelists are not worthy of the name. But, again, I have fallen into the muddy ditch.

10. The Artist's Ideal
In fact, our lecture, the purpose of which was to speak to you about literature, has not yet progressed. In explaining the operations of differentiation, it just followed naturally to talk about men of letters and so I addressed the problem of a novelist's skill in discernment. All in all, taking account of what I have written on this subject, I cannot say that the men of letters have fulfilled

their mission. As I have previously emphasized, without recourse to appropriate differentiation they can fulfill only a part of their purpose. Consequently, in giving a lecture that proposes to cover all literature, one is obliged to proceed in a somewhat recapitulative manner. From now on, I will direct myself towards this end.

In each operation of differentiation, we effect a separation between the Ego and the objects and beings outside ourselves. We differentiate between external objects or beings by nature, human beings (taken as beings outside ourselves) and supernatural divinities (that is, when we recognize the existence of independent divinities). We differentiate ourselves into three elements: intelligence, perception and will. When we connect these three factors to the beings or objects outside ourselves, three distinct things can happen: individuals can cause their intelligence to be exercised in relation to objects or beings outside themselves, or their perception to be exercised in relation to outside objects or beings, or their will to be exercised in relation to outside objects or beings. Of course, as these operations do not originate in isolation, the statement that one causes intelligence, perception and will to be exercised, should in no way be taken to mean that we exclude other operations and that we exercise only these three. But we can identify from these operations three categories of individuals: those who cause their intelligence to be exercised are people who have a clear understanding of our relationships with objects and beings outside ourselves; we normally call them philosophers or scientists. Those who cause their perception to be exercised are people who appreciate relationships with outside objects and beings with enthusiasm; we normally call them men of letters or artists. Finally, those who exercise their will to reform relationships with outside objects and beings are normally called soldiers, politicians, tofu merchants or even carpenters.

When we thus differentiate the content of awareness,

since the development of this content also becomes extremely varied—because of this ideal about which I was talking previously—it is difficult to know what could emerge from this continuity of awareness. Whatever it may be, a large area of choice becomes available, which is significant in that it informs the development of the Ego. An individual with a continuity of awareness that leads him to focus on exercising his perception in relation to an ideal that is defined as a thirst for life, will ultimately become a man of letters, a painter or a musician. Similarly, the great majority of those who develop a continuity of awareness that leads them to exercise strong willpower will become, as a result, farmers or rickshaw pullers, and this is not a minor matter; they sign up for the army, throw themselves into adventures or stir up revolutions.

We can broadly divide the ideal of human beings into three categories. As far as we are concerned, in the positions that we occupy today—I myself, who have the great honor of giving this lecture, and you, who have the goodness to listen to it—if we are asked which category our ideal belongs to, it goes without saying that it belongs to the second. This is not to say that, as we can exercise our perception and we wish to live, we do not wish to exercise either our intelligence or our will. However, our ideal implies that, if we diverge from our concentration on perception, we will no longer wish to stay alive. But the statement "Perception is our ideal" is unconvincing. To be convinced of it, when I say to you "Yes, in fact, we must go into a little detail today and make perception our ideal," and when you say to me, "Yes, that is right," then it seems that I must provide a detailed analysis in my speech. I said that people who exercise their perception appreciate relationships with objects or beings with enthusiasm. Since those who behave in this way can do so only if they clearly perceive relationships with objects or beings, and in some cases refashion those relationships, people with perception must already have intelligence and will, and it goes without saying that a man of letters must be at one and the same time a philosopher and a person of a practical turn of mind (a creator). However, people who are particularly gifted in perceiving relationships clearly, who can perceive them much more easily than others, may then abstract them to such a point that it is impossible for them to appreciate the relationships with enthusiasm. When we have three apples, and we say that it is good for this relationship to appear very clearly formed by the number 3, we forget the apples, which are the essential component, and we begin to attach importance only to the number 3. It is essential for men of letters to be able to perceive these relationships clearly, since the act of perceiving them clearly is dictated by the objective of being able to appreciate them better than before. But, however much we say that a perception is clear, if one is incapable of appreciating these relationships, however clearly they are perceived, nothing results. In the example of the three apples, the awareness of a relationship that is defined by the number 3 is sufficient, but it is impossible for a writer to forget that it is really a question of a fruit called an apple. A similar argument can be made when a writer causes his will to be exercised. Refashioning relationships with objects and beings is not an aim in itself, and one undertakes this work of reformation to enable a better exercise of perception. When perception is ignored, the fact of reforming relationships prevents the writer from exercising his judgment. Placing a few stones near a pine tree as a kind of decoration is a physical thing, but cutting down the pine and going to sell it at the public baths presents difficulties. When the pine has disappeared in puffs of smoke, there is no longer any way to perceive it. To examine this in detail, as far as men of letters and artists are concerned, it would seem that the meaning of the phrase "appreciating relationships with objects and beings with enthusiasm" has become slightly clearer. We know that, for it to be possible to appreciate objects and beings with enthusiasm, they must take on a concrete form; and as soon as, through the application of intelligence and will, we break the concrete form of the object or the being by blows, it becomes impossible for men of letters to appreciate it with enthusiasm. Therefore, in accordance with the need for this concrete form, which displays physical attributes and allows perception to be exercised, men of letters exercise intelligence and will without destroying the concrete state of the object or being. This is what happens first.

11. The Ideal of the Man of Letters and the Artist: The Aesthetic Ideal

Therefore, if the ideal of a man of letters or an artist is entirely separate from what is perceptible, it cannot be realized. If we look at the subject in detail, various questions arise, but as we do not have the time for this I shall not go into it. I am sure that this will be acceptable to you, given that I have already explained the essential points. My suggestions are hastily made, but when you want to write, draw or paint God, who is odorless and intangible, you will never produce a text or painting unless you borrow from something perceptible. So, the God who is found in the Old Testament and the Greek divinities all have a voice, form or some other perceptible feature. This is why I think that the ideal of a man of letters or an artist, such as ourselves, expresses a certain form of perception through the intermediary of something that can be perceived. Two problems therefore arise: (1) What constitutes something that is perceptible? (2) To what aspect of the thing that is perceptible does this factor belong and how can it be explained? Is it "the intermediary of something that can be perceived" that makes representation possible or is it the object itself that gives rise to its expression? When you can explain these problems, you will have achieved a good understanding of the conditions of differentiation of the ideal of the man of letters. I do not say that it is necessary to explain the first problem, then the second, in that order. If you prefer an order to facilitate your comprehension, well, by saying number 1, then 2, I will proceed to explain. I have said that through the construction of time and space we have created a double world made up of things and beings outside ourselves, and our Ego. I said that what appeared to be objects or beings outside ourselves comprised nature, other people (perceived as beings outside ourselves), God or divinities (if they exist outside ourselves). Although God and the divinities do not a have a perceptible form, they do not present a problem in this respect. When God appears to a man of letters or an artist, he perceives God as a perceptible object, and also as an apparition, and so we can include it in the same system of classification as the other items. With regard to nature and human beings, we experience a form of perception. In other words, faced with all the elements in these perceptible human beings or this perceptible nature, whether they be nuances of colors, combinations of lines, proportions, suppleness or hardness, the way they reflect the light, voices in nature or of human beings, we experience enthusiasm and, as a result, love or aversion. Thus, it is possible to appreciate these perceptible elements (nature and human beings) with enthusiasm. Moreover, we want to be aware of the more remarkable relationships among them. As mediums for realizing this ideal, that is, for achieving this awareness of relationships, there are poetry and painting. In the context of this ideal, we experience what we call our "aesthetic response," which is the most remarkable element of perception. (In reality, beyond this aesthetic ideal, other ideals arise. One can respond to a given object as a "sheer profile, rising very high" or as a "carefree bohemian spirit." And there is no problem in being able to understand that one aesthetic response to the object will be to see it as a sheer profile and the other will be to see it as representing the bohemian free spirit. Acts of differentiation naturally lead to these forms of aesthetic response. But because of beauty or aesthetics, an idea advanced by Westerners, we are plunged into great difficulty.) The desire to realize an ideal of this kind in response to the natural world is achieved through landscape painting or even through a Chinese or Japanese poet composing haiku, and taking pleasure in depicting the landscapes of the world. Then again, when one wants to realize this ideal in response to human relationships, one becomes a poet wanting to depict beautiful women or a painter. Nowadays, we make a lot of fuss, both in the West and in Japan, about the painting of nudes, for example, and this calls for a great effort to be made so that we can constitute an ideal in this area, which is to be considered as the objective of a whole life. Is it perhaps difficult at the technical level? But if we look at it from the perspective of the ideal of the man of letters or artist, this can only be a part of it. Someone said that an artist painted nudes only when he had reached the final phase of the genius of painting. As I am not a connoisseur of painting, I am unable to comment on this, but it seems to me that the paint-ing of nudes is a result of the revival in the Orient of a method current in France today. In any case, it does not much matter whether it is a question of painting, poetry or prose. Since, hav-ing put aside the fact that human beings, who are considered as perceptible objects, constitute only a part of all the objects that are perceptible, it is clear that what we call the "aesthetic response" is only a part of the aesthetic response relating to human beings taken as perceptible objects. What we call the aes-thetics of the nude is perhaps admirable, but it seems to me that it is only a narrow area.

Since the problem consists of choosing by the method of appreciation of the moment how one perceives the relationships among us all and the things or beings outside us, one of the three available methods—the aesthetic response, the abrupt response or the carefree response appropriate to the bohem-ian—must be governed by the ideal of the artist, if the ideal which results from the process of differentiation is developed.

I do not know up to what point fragmentation can be effected. However, whatever the number of fragmentations, the ideal I am talking about here springs from these types of relationship when one has seen perceptible objects as perceptible objects. Having taken account of the fact that the aesthetic response occurs at the moment one sees a perceptible object, it remains to be discovered whether, by using such objects as instruments to attain, through their mediation, an aesthetic goal, this kind of response should not be confused with an aesthetic response to something which has no perceptible form.

12. The Artist's Ideal (1): The Ideal in Contact with Love and Morality

I think that you have broadly understood what I have said to you regarding the ideal and the aesthetic response in relation to external objects and to the Ego. I have talked about objects, but have not yet discussed the Ego. So now, as this time the Ego has priority, I will talk a little about it.

(1) If we break down actions originating from the Ego into intelligence, perception and will, as I outlined previously, a person who, on the basis of intelligence, has the task of shedding light on relationships between external beings or objects is called a philosopher or a scientist. If we place ourselves at the level of what we call "shedding light on relationships," this is a task, without any doubt, that falls within the area chosen by philosophers. However, to shed light on these relationships, taking the hypothesis that a particular form of perception occurs, in spite of the intervention of intelligence, I wonder whether one should discuss literary or artistic actions here in relation to the "appearance" of this perception. Now, as I have previously explained, in order to satisfy our perception while exercising our intelligence, a process of abstraction occurs that causes relationships to emerge between objects or beings outside the Ego, separate from their perceptible existence. In other words, in

exercising intelligence in an artistic manner, unless we have recourse to a sensory element we will not manage to construct anything at all. The action of intelligence can produce an artistic or cultural creation through a real object or through the mediation of a real object. And while this is taking place, a new ideal, founded on a literary or artistic approach, makes its appearance. Therefore, in using an object or being outside ourselves as a tool, and exercising intelligence and clarifying relationships, an ideal appears which allows perception to be achieved. We say that this ideal is directly related to Truth. Consequently, this ideal, in direct relation to Truth, is both the domain of the philosopher or scientist and that of the man of letters or artist. However, when men of letters or artists make Truth appear through real elements, they are behaving differently from philosophers or scientists. Therefore, the method of making Truth appear, and so the conditions under which we exercise intelligence, come to be differentiated and different results are achieved. However, the mental activities of human beings (in this context I do not consider human beings to be pure perceptible objects, as defined above) are largely employed in situations that have developed either in concert with the laws of causality that we have determined in advance or in accordance with a new significance that adds another differentiation to the laws of causality. For example, when a heated discussion occurs between a father and his child, a conflagration breaks out very quickly; the house is filled with smoke. Then the child who started the violent altercation rapidly forgets the quarrel it had with its father. They help each other. Then the child runs off and disappears. This is the type of story we tell in novels. The novelist who writes this story, and the readers, say to each other, "Of course these kinds of things can easily happen in real life." As a result, this novel, by shedding light on the relationship between father and child under certain circumstances, and by allowing the intelligence of author and reader to be exercised, provides a perception relating to Truth. In the same way, a married couple who go perfectly with each other forget during a period of hunger the love that normally reigns between them. The husband steals the rice gruel from his wife, which she wanted to eat, and a novel is written based on this story of the husband having eaten the rice. In this case, too, by shedding light on conjugal relationships under certain circumstances, perhaps there will be mutual satisfaction on the part of author and reader. (In terms of the psychology of human beings, Truth varies. Sometimes, in spite of contrasting views, there can be Truth on both sides.) We call a man an artist who professes Truth as an ideal and who deliberately draws or depicts such relationships.

(2) The second factor that allows us to exercise our mental faculties is perception. We have already said that we call men of letters those whose ideal consists in the exercise of this ability to perceive. But, having explained this, confusion can easily arise when we attempt to draw conclusions, and so I will move on even though I have only spoken a little on this subject. The word "perception" in itself is ambiguous. To exercise our perceptive ability, we create literary or artistic works. What allows us to create such works and comes into play in our aesthetic appreciation must be distinguished from what we use to perceive the form of the objects we use in a work. When we consider perceptible objects as perceptible objects, we exercise a specific form of our perceptive ability. This process constitutes one of the artist's ideals. When we exercise our intelligence, by relating objects to each other, a particular kind of perception comes into play. And this type of perception also represents an ideal for the artist. And when we exercise our perception through the intermediary of a perceptible object, we should be able to identify another kind of perception. As far as these two different types of perception are concerned, even if they equate in terms of content, if one ignores their individual identity and the uniqueness of their

nature, only total confusion can result. For example, if we show an emotion that we call "anger" as a result of a certain perceptible object that we ourselves experience, as opposed to anger represented in a literary or artistic work, however much it may be the same kind of anger, the two kinds of anger are different. The anger in the first case is the cause, and in the second case it is the effect. To put this more simply, the first form of anger derives from direct contact with perceptible objects (even if the source of this emotion comes from the fact that I spread the anger that stirs me up to beings other than myself), whilst the second occurs entirely within the individual that we call the Ego. So, to avoid confusion, let us proceed by taking care to separate these two forms of perception. However, regarding the logic of my argument, the first case we looked at shows that we love to exercise our intelligence and there is no difference between this fact and what I have explained just now regarding forms of perception. The emotions that come and go within the heart, sadness and joy, pain and pleasure, not only constitute in themselves the greatest part of our awareness but also, at times when we recognize something objectively and in beings outside ourselves (among whom we find human beings in many cases) considerably stimulate our perceptive capacity. However, we can profit from such stimulation only when our emotions, based on the conditions I have described, arise in response to aspects of the real world and, particularly, to human beings. If people who we assume are interested in the process of perception, such as psychologists, deal with it in abstract terms, it is impossible that anything artistic can result. However, in so far as the subject to which we allude consists only of emotions, which can be dealt with in abstract terms more easily than intelligence or will, it is impossible to say that this could not become a subject outside ourselves. However, as I do not have time to explain this to you in detail, I am going to cut short my remarks.

13. The Artist's Ideal (2): The Ideal Compared with Morality and the Ideal of the Sublime

Therefore, whatever ideal we attain, the results of the operations of differentiation are varied. Firstly, if we talk about elements that serve as standards, let us take beings or objects that are other than ourselves (but rather than talking generally about beings or objects different from us, our understanding will be assisted if we deal with humans, so I am going to talk about people), so, let us take eight or nine so-called novelists who have set themselves the task of depicting romantic relationships, as an ideal. When we differentiate this type of relationship, we find many different forms. There are people who love each other and get married. There are those who contract the illness of love. However, in some recent novels, such old themes seem to have become rarefied. The tone is more cutting. If a woman is married, she cherishes a warm affection for another man. Or couples find that the passion that brought them together has been satiated and start to quarrel the day after their marriage. Different ideals arise—but it seems funny to discuss ideals in this context. In any case, there are different kinds. Further, the main moral feelings that constitute the basis of virtue, fidelity, filial devotion, chivalry and friendship, going hand in hand with those changes that originated from differentiation, have all become standardized norms. Using a generalization to describe these moral feelings in a normalized form, the expression "ideal of Goodness" comes into play. I should like to talk to you about this in more detail, but as time presses I will cut this discussion short and pass on to the next subject.

(3) The third form of mental operation is represented by the will. For the artistic expression of the will, its manifestation through the medium of a perceptible object or being is essential. So, the perceptible object or being serves as an instrument and full light is shed on the operation of the will. However, to

what extent is this instrument an instrument? Apart from its function in the manifestation of will, the object itself has its own intrinsic value. Take, for example an object, a jug of saké; I would not wish to deny that it can be an object of value in itself. However, if there is a hole in the bottom of the jug, we cannot prevent the saké leaking out. In that case, it is impossible for the jug to fulfill its proper role among the various pieces of crockery and to fulfill the wishes of the master of the house. Let us now imagine a large cannonball that flies into the sky. There are two ways of perceiving it. The first way is simply to see a perceptible object; and this belongs to the first category that I mentioned earlier. The second way is to perceive the great force deployed through the intermediary of this perceptible object. But it is impossible to depict this force in isolation, and so the cannonball in itself is not the most important thing and the true aim of the artist is to express the force produced by it. Under the combined effect of nature and mechanics, a particular form of the operation of the will is demonstrated. When we see people climbing Mount Fuji in winter, we say they are mad. Yes, there is no doubt, they are stupid. However, if we accept that a certain willpower is reflected in their stupidity, we do not need to focus on their stupidity, and if we are interested only in the manifestation of this willpower and the appearance of elements of an artistic nature, that is perhaps a good thing. The idiots who swim the Channel or cross the Sahara, and risk their lives to achieve a continuity of awareness that will allow them to exercise their willpower, offer something else as a sacrifice. As a result, if we depict this in a purely artistic way, it will unquestionably become a work of art. This is all the more so if the will is developed through a combination of the great moral emotions of which I have spoken; whether one acts for the Motherland, The Way or the human race, noble emotions become apparent. At such times, these emotions give new strength to people struck down by cowardice.[12] In English we call this *heroism*. Undoubtedly, we consider heroism to be something noble and prodigious. When I arrived here, I caught sight of large billows of smoke escaping inconsiderately from the high chimneys of the Arsenal[13] going straight up into the sky. I found the sight particularly impressive. When one thinks about it, soot and equivalent substances are trivial things. If we want to talk about dirt in this world below, well, it is difficult to find anything dirtier than coal burning. And if I find that all this soot emitted by this smoke comes from the exhalation of the smoke by the chimney, which declares that it is going to earn a lot of money, it is even more repugnant. In addition, this smoke is no good for lung diseases. However, forgetting this type of problem, I feel a particular emotion. In other words, it seems to me that in one sense we have here a manifestation of will.[14] The smoke that escapes from the Arsenal being what it is, if one is on the side of authentic heroism, well, I think that there is a true feeling of heroism. There are hardly any artists today who would describe this kind of feeling as ideal. It goes without saying that one can proceed to differentiate within this ideal. Nanko Mashasige,[15] whilst committing suicide with his brother at Minatogawa,[16] one killing the other, uttered the following words: "If God wishes, while I am human, I will exterminate

---

[12] Reference to a quotation from the Chinese thinker Mencius. Mencius (Mengzi, "Master Meng") lived in the second half of the fourteenth century. Like Confucius, he was from the Lu country.

[13] This factory was situated in Tokyo in the Koishikawa district (today Bunkyo-ku suburb, Kōraku district). It was a weapons factory, strategic for the army.

[14] Whatever the inconvenience that such a factory might cause, in particular provoking lung diseases because of emissions of soot, it would seem that, for the author, one could detect in it a manifestation of the will responding to the moral ideal of the love of one's country, evoking a specific heroism. Would it not also be appropriate to detect a note of irony, usual in this writer, in this remark?

many times more the criminals who are the enemies of the Emperor."This is an example of heroic conduct. Here is another. Daito Kokushi[17] was lame and he could not sit with his legs crossed. When his last hour came, he folded with a sinister crack the leg which troubled him, giving it the following message: "Do what I tell you!" and, indifferent to the fresh blood that stained his priestly robe, he expired in the za-zen position. If we differentiate heroism, various situations appear. However, at the normative level, it is possible to state, in my humble opinion, that the emotion of the Sublime dominates these two acts.

14. Relationships between the Artistic Ideal and Time, between the Artistic Ideal and Individuals: Four Categories of Values for the Ideal

Now, let us first introduce a general classification for categories of those ideals that are deployed at the artistic level, and their elucidation. If I may summarize briefly, (1) the perceptible object taken as such is confronted by emotions (the representation of which is the aesthetic ideal); (2) where the three operations, originating from intelligence, perception and will are exercised through the intermediary of a perceptible object, these processes are divided as follows: (a) the case in which one exercises intelligence (represented by the ideal of Truth); (b) the case in which one exercises perception (represented by the ideal of love or moral virtue); and (c) the case in which one exercises will (represented by the ideal of the Sublime). We really ought

---

[15] Kusunoki Masashige (1294–1336). In response to a request from the Emperor Godaigo (1288–1339), who ascended the throne in 1318 and was trying to regain power, he raised an army and fought against the Shogun of Kamakura.

[16] Minatogawa, a river with its mouth in the town of Kobe.

[17] Daitō Kokushi (1282–1337), a priest of the Zen Riazi Buddhist sect, who lived at the Daitokuji temple, the principle temple of the Rinzai sect in the Murakasino district in the north of Kyoto.

to discuss here whether emotions, originating from the association of ideas, should be mixed in some way on the basis of these
four broad categories. But I have no time for this either; I will
call a halt on this subject too.

I have finally managed to divide the artist's ideal into these
four categories. In my "Essay on Literature," I described this
classification slightly differently. But there is nothing to be done
about that, as the starting point is different. However, as the
method of classification that I am showing you here seems clear
and appropriate, whatever the differences between the two, they
will not present any problem for you, gentlemen. So, as I said
before, despite the fact that our mental operations, which originate from intelligence, perception and will, can be differentiated, if they remain in a state of isolation from one another,
they cannot be manifested in any way. Furthermore, at the artistic level, given that all these operations are revealed by the intermediary of perceptible objects or beings, and that feelings and
emotions also in these four categories of ideal mingle with each
other and become more complex, in reality the four ideals do
not originate in a work clearly divided in this way. Nevertheless,
there are four distinct categories of ideal and it is impossible to
reduce that number. In addition, if we take a given work and
examine it, one of these four categories will stand out more
clearly than the others. Thus, the problem of determining the
category of ideal that applies to the work can be dealt with only
to a limited extent. Therefore, the fact that these four categories
of ideal suffer the ups and downs of life, on which the energy
of ideals is exercised, and which vary according to different
periods and individuals, is a reality that is beyond doubt. In a
certain period, we go so far as to consider that there is no artistic achievement if we do not satisfy the requirements of Beauty.
In the following period, the ideal changes and we feel that,
rather than Beauty, if we do not show Truth our creations do

not justify the reward of the two characters that signify "art and letters." Someone may also affirm that he does not want to create, or read a work or do anything that does not succeed in satisfying the moral sense. Someone else may go so far as to claim that, if we do not succeed in expressing the emotion of the Sublime, which accompanies the manifestation of the will, we do not feel that we are appreciating something artistic. The periods to which these four categories of ideal refer, as well as the people connected with them, represent something totally precise. And if someone says that any one of these four categories of ideal is appropriate, and that it does not matter which, then I think that we can say that this is an opinion that might be held by broader-minded and more reasonable people. What are the prevalent categories during a particular period? Which are most welcomed by this type of person? These questions are of greater interest, but again I do not have enough time, and so I will cut this discussion short. I would like to say a few words also on the following subject. These four categories of ideal, as their names indicate, profess ideas that are in harmony with each other; that is how they become artistic ideals. This is why it is impossible to say what causes a given category of ideal to be subject to another. As there are degrees of importance within these categories, one could say that for certain periods we were going to attempt to measure this difference by allocating points. I think that it is impossible that anyone would be bold enough to do so. To do this would be equivalent to a teacher, having lost his common sense, marking an examination without looking at the answers given by the students, and therefore understanding nothing. I cannot find appropriate words to ex-press this. But as we are under pressure of time, if we say that we like this or that ideal, this is entirely appropriate. If we wish to choose an orientation that is included in this or that ideal according to our individuality, this is worthy of indulgence.

As sympathies or antipathies are not subject to reason, it is still possible for us to say that we like or hate something. But if we are uncomfortable in making these sympathies and antipathies known, without any foundation, our attempt to justify our preference in an area in which we cannot reason will be like saying that we do not like octopus when the reason is that one has poor digestion. If it were our favorite food, it would seem that, whatever our incapacity to digest it, we would happily eat all the tentacles.

15. The Value of the Four Categories of Ideal

For this reason, the four categories of ideal have the same prerogatives, which are exercised in a reciprocal manner and according to the rule that they must not clash with each other. Therefore, focusing exclusively on Beauty and arguing about it seems to me like a bad move in a game of *Shōgi* where the rook has the king in check. It is exactly as if we judged people's appetite by taking as a standard the time they get up. No one would willingly submit himself to such a peremptory judgment as, "You, friend, you like to lie in all morning; so, as you do nothing in bed all morning, you eat immoderately." If you take a saké measure to measure a piece of fabric and you order someone to measure a remnant of material, no one will do it for you with that utensil. If people, looking at a thermometer, say, "Oh, this mountain is really high!" I advise them to measure the degree of fury that will result if they mistake an ordinary thermometer for a medical thermometer; you can only leave them to it, in my opinion. If I give a critical judgment on errors of appreciation, when we look at works in which Beauty has been revealed, I do not deny that Truth is absent in this process. We criticize here suggestions of this type: "In the absence of Truth, it is a failure; it cannot become a work of art." Perhaps Truth is absent from the work, but then so much the better! I doubt that anyone will say he wants something that it is said does not exist.

But, if at the same time we do not manage to see at least the Beauty that exists in reality, then the life of the work really does come to an end. If you say, "Your head is bald, but only your beard is white!," this is fair (impartial). However, if you brush this aside by retorting, "It is not your bald head I want to talk to you about," this beard is a real disaster. The two statues[18] carved by Unkei,[19] representing King Deva's guards, express the will in movement. But I think it is impossible to analyze their anatomy precisely. In criticisms of Unkei's works, it has been noted that they are unrealistic; well, when one says that "these works are poor," the way of saying it is in itself bad. Millet's painting "The Angelus,"[20] expresses a specific feeling of distance. If we are interested in this subject, we can identify various aspects of it. And if people say that there is no movement of will in that painting, it is best just to listen to such remarks and put up with them patiently. If someone declared that it could not be considered a picture because of the absence of movement of will, that would be such a pointless judgment that they might as well be a frog gazing at a work of art.

However, when expressing a certain type of ideal, there is a slight difference between the cases in which other ideals are absent and those in which, in the name of our own ideal, we actively attack and demolish another ideal. While the absence of an ideal means simply that it is not included, the action of demolishing an alternative ideal is an affront to that ideal. In that case, the ideal the writer has chosen as his standard should be represented in the work in a sufficiently ingenious manner to

---

[18] The two statues (*nio*), representing the guardians of the God Deva "Vajrapani," are those of a generally frightening appearance that one often sees on either side of the entrance to a Buddhist temple.

[19] Unkei (?–1222), a famous sculpture in the early Kamakura period.

[20] The painting by Jean-François Millet (1814–1875), very popular for a long time, was often appreciated for social or moral reasons, but rarely, until recent art criticism, for its artistic merit.

cause the other ideals to be forgotten. But, even with genius, this is extremely difficult. Normally, the qualities and defects cancel each other out, and the balance that remains is simply deleted by drawing a line through it. Think of "yokan" pastry from the Fujimura[21] cake shop; let us suppose that we put this delicacy in a chamber pot. Well, such a thing makes me hesitate. To be indifferent as to whether the "yokan" is or is not in the chamber pot and to go on and devour it greedily, it is essential to have an unconditional enthusiasm for it. Take also the example of someone with the required academic qualifications who is determined to become a teacher. Well, if we were to find that he was leading a completely dissolute life, his application would be refused without appeal. If we were prepared to be satisfied with the acknowledgment that his conduct was not irreproachable, his application might succeed! But if, after a frantic spree in the red light district, he returned reeling to his school, hiding in his pocket a bill over two feet long, such a spectacle could not but have a certain impact on the good reputation that the educational establishment enjoyed. So, whatever its merits and faults, if the merits alone are insufficient to enable the faults to be overlooked, a literary work, however regrettable it may be, will not receive a favorable welcome. I wish particularly to emphasize the phrase that I used just now—"however regrettable it may be." What one can regret is that this is already a literary criticism based on the recognition of the merits and, at the same time, another criticism founded on a perfect knowledge of the defects. And as I have no wish to go at the same rate as Panurge's sheep, the sheep in front uniformly pushing the sheep behind for five or six years, I shall express myself in this way.

---

[21] At the end of the twelfth century, the power of the Fujiwara was waning and Japan experienced large social upheavals that ended in the victory of Minamoto no Yoritomo (1185) and the establishment of the military government, the Bakufu, in Kamakura.

16. The Ideal of the Contemporary Man of Letters (1): The Ideal of Truth

Now, finally moving on to the ideal of contemporary letters and arts, I should like to make some fairly grandiloquent remarks. What, then, is the predominant ideal in our contemporary letters and arts? Beauty? No, not Beauty! In painting or sculpture, does Beauty, expressed in all its purity, perhaps exist? But as I do not know about the subject, I will not worry you about it. If I talk about Beauty in literature, I can say that it is completely absent. What we might see as the uniting of Beauty with life does not exist in my opinion, outside short poems. As for novels, it goes without saying that it is absent. It is the same, of course, in dramatic texts (plays or operas). As it would take time to go into detail, in spite of the annoyance that this will cause you, for which I request you please to excuse me, I am going to submit my exposition. The contemporary ideal not being Beauty, would it consist of Good or Love? An ideal of this type surely has a texture, comprising weft and warp. However, it is truly too weak for us to say that it represents the contemporary ideal. So, would the ideal be the Sublime? If this were the incarnation of the contemporary ideal, it would not be very promising for the future. But, in reality, completely the opposite is the case. In my opinion, acts of heroism are more scarce in the contemporary world than at any other period in history and literature which accentuates the emotion of the Sublime is rare. We well understand, therefore, that there is no single tragedy in the contemporary world that displays qualities of grandeur. Since the ideal of the contemporary world does not consist of Beauty, Good or the idea of the Sublime, our conclusion must be that the contemporary ideal resides in an ideogram meaning "Truth." If we want to provide examples, it will take a long time; if we want proof, it will be difficult. As we cannot do anything about it, we can say that it is only Truth that comprises the ideal of arts and letters, and most particularly that of literature.

I would like you to tell me whether this corresponds in your opinion to reality. Now, what represents this ideal of Truth can surely, through the supposed process of differentiation, be divided into various categories and levels. If one reads deeply all the works of English, French, German or Russian literature, it is possible to identify major variations. Personally, I have no intention of complaining about this. As I said before, Truth is one of the four ideals. This ideal has gained in strength and the other ideals have, by comparison, lost the popularity they once had. We may think this is inevitable and dependent on the course of events, in the same way as the traditional feminine hairstyle, with the hair in a fan,[22] has been abandoned, according to changes in taste, in favor of the bun[23] which is now fashionable. However, to say something on this subject that you can use as reference, I will continue as follows.

Take human observation. Well, the deeper it becomes, the narrower it becomes. I use the word "narrow": we cannot find anyone narrower in the entire world than so-called "specialists." As what I understand by "narrow" has no particularly derogatory significance, perhaps you will say that this is unimportant. But the coverage of the term "narrow" does include aspects of the specialist that are annoying. When a doctor is excessively zealous in his science and cannot keep the narrow range of his speciality out of his head, whether he is awake or asleep, he ends up by giving his wife a toxic drug to drink and tries to experiment from the results obtained. The world is wide! In this vast space to stretch out a cotton thread, to walk cautiously on it without turning aside one's eyes and to mistake this for the whole world is pathetic in itself. If it is no more than pathetic,

---

[22] *Ichōgaeshi*, a woman's hairstyle in the shape of a fan, fashionable from the end of the Edo period until the Meiji era. It is quoted in Sōseki's *The Three-Cornered World* (1906).

[23] *Sokuhatsu*, a Western hairstyle in a bun, fashionable in the Meiji and Taishō eras. In 1885, an association was established to popularize the hairstyle.

and the person in question puts up with the situation, this is an end to the matter. But however much we walk monotonously like this, we are very much hindered by the surrounding world. Here I refer also to the literal action of walking in the street. However much the policeman wants to manage the situation by shouting as loud as the man who counts hours worked to calculate wages, "Go left! Go left!," it is impossible to manipulate people who are going every which way into a single straight line, in the same direction and at the same speed. If the human beings who live in this wide world cover wide areas at the rate they wish, in a direction that suits their taste, when they pass each other on the road and collisions occur between them, it is essential, unless there is a particular reason against it, to make mutual concessions. The four types of the ideal, each having equal rights, direct their existence. The chosen route is subject to the free will of each individual, but as equality of rights is determined in advance, when collisions occur both parties must strive for an amicable settlement and absolutely must reach an understanding. If, in our attempt to conclude this agreement, we see only our own point of view and we follow only our own path, then a successful outcome will be impossible. In short, we must have sufficient generosity to recognize that men, from near or far, all have different and worthy occupations and have good reasons for their choice. Now, if the sphere of interest is narrowed and deepened, as in the example of the doctor I mentioned just now, this generosity becomes impossible. And when we talk about laws of extraction, if we fix our gaze exclusively on the object of our passion, neglecting everything else, this means that we put other things completely aside. We take no notice of them. Other items can no longer, because of this mental attitude, enter the field of vision. Such a situation may, in fact, be a blessing for the person concerned, but for others—that is to say, for those who are not going in the same direction—it causes great disruption. If we feel that such inconvenience will occur, we must find palliatives. But if a situation comes about because of the shrinking of the world perceived by the Ego, and the consequent lack of appreciation that other people inhabit a world distinct from its tight space, it will be impossible to do anything whatsoever. I wonder if the harm caused to arts and letters by the excessive importance granted to Good is not an example of what I have just described. Well, I think that this is, in fact, the case.

17. The Ideal of the Contemporary Man of Letters (2): The Preponderance Accorded to the Ideal of Truth

When we favor Truth, from the moment we reach Truth what we write is no longer very important. If, as a consequence of showing Truth ostentatiously, Beauty, Good and the ideal of the Sublime are regarded as negligible, so be it; but if we then take one step too many in favoring Truth, we will alter Beauty, we will harm Good, we will trample on the ideal of the Sublime. People who belong to the faction that defends Truth would perhaps cheer, but it would be impossible, I believe, for those assembled under the banners of Good, Beautiful and the ideal of the Sublime, feeling resentment as an opportunity passes under their noses, to go back underground while telling the representatives of Truth that they were right. To declare that everything comes from the fact that our aims are different from each other would be equivalent to saying that it is within the sphere of all our interests not to harm others. And when people who do not cause trouble for others, not recognizing that things which do not exercise influence on them can have a stable existence, come and proclaim everywhere "We are in the world of Truth! We are in the world of Truth!," this is just like stating in public, "We live in a world remarkable for its convenience of transport." The tram, whose driver rings his bell with all his might, travels like a mad thing along the road that fancy makes us choose. People with a predilection for this form of transport, considering it impossible to travel if one does not take the tram, might perhaps be satisfied with this; but I think that for those who travel on foot, who take a means of transport powered by human energy, who go by bicycle, there is nothing more unpleasant.

However, as far as arts and letters are concerned, whether on the level of appreciation or on that of creation, they contain a certain number of "rules of extraction." (As I have discussed these rules in my essay on literature, I invite you to refer to it.) When we reach these extremities, strange phenomena appear. For example, this painting of a nude of which I spoke is exhibited to the public in the light of day. If one agrees with the point of view dictated by social morality, the nude is something indecent that offends the sight; and if a Westerner expressed himself on the subject, his opinion would not be particularly different—I guarantee it. However, to bring out the perceptible beauty of the human body, we must unquestionably paint nudes. We must then overcome the aspect of indecency. And this is where the conflict arises. This conflict, as civilization progresses, becomes increasingly bitter and we cannot resolve it; and this situation has developed to such an extent that no mediation seems possible; to reach a compromise, one of two things is necessary: either change the habits of society or renounce the perceptible beauty of our physical form. But as these two options are both proof of stubbornness, we have adopted a form of contradictory commitment with the purpose of bringing to a conclusion at all costs something for which an arrangement is difficult to find. An appropriate commitment might be presented in the form, "As much as one is struck by the perceptible beauty of the flesh, one must forget the social impropriety of the nude!" If we make use of this difficult approach, we must look at paintings of nudes and "extract" the feeling of indecency. Having declared such a commitment, it becomes possible for the painting of nudes to extend our perception of life and so, as certain artists or critics think, there is no reason to take a high and mighty stance towards this genre. This is very like the tram. Companies such as Totetsu or Denetsu may well operate in a situation in which passengers forget to extract the idea of danger in relation to a particular itinerary, since this method of transport is comfortable despite the danger it presents. If the equivalents of Totetsu or Denetsu in the painting of nudes show too much arrogance, it would be best to take away their right to existence. However, once a commitment to operate a process of extraction has been concluded, there are no more problems. It is the same with Truth. In works that highlight Truth, all other ideals are forgotten. When we forget other ideals, we have made an abstraction of them; when we discuss works that express the ideal of Truth, we forget other ideals, but this is the way it goes. When I say that this is the way it goes, I am not saying that the works that highlight Truth have a high and mighty air. Truth can exist; I say that this is the way it goes. Gentlemen of other ideals, this will annoy you; it annoys me, too, but be patient! If we maintain this attitude of reserve, there will be no problems. However, in order to create similar conditions, it would be essential to use our ingenuity to show our feelings about Truth so that they would achieve such intensity as to cause our other ideals to be forgotten. I doubt that such a manner of operating is possible in contemporary works.

As my argument has become far too abstract, I will attempt to illustrate my thoughts a little with an example. Let us take someone who pretends to be dumb. Suspected of some misdeed, he is arrested by the police. Realizing that it could be prejudicial to answer questions when he is interrogated, he pretends to be stupid and dumb. The police are therefore obliged to leave him alone. The next morning, our mute is seized by an intense hunger. At first, as he is dumb, he is patient and says nothing. But at last he can contain his hunger no longer and he bursts out, "For pity's sake, give me something to eat!" If we write something using such a trick as a departure, what will come of it? The skill that would enable us to write an engrossing novel would give us the opportunity to express a variety of Truths related to the subject—concerning a certain type of character, and referring to various circumstances. I think the interest lies in that. However, that is all there is and Beauty, Good and the ideal of the Sublime are absent from it. That is to say, apart from Truth it contains no other ideal. If we ask whether that is a defect, I would not see it as such in this case. Even if this type of work contains no other ideal, this does not harm it in any way. Thus, the fact of experiencing only an interest in the work that is connected to Truth, and abstracting all other ideals, makes it possible to read it up to the end.

18. The Ideal of the Contemporary Man of Letters (3): The Predominance Accorded to the Ideal of Truth

Then, if we write the following story, what will happen? A tramp, wandering from place to place, is tormented by hunger. When he appears on a certain day and at a certain time in a certain village, he goes up to a building where, by chance, everything is quiet. Seeing that there is no living soul around, he steals some bread and wine. After eating his fill, he goes to the edge of the village. He feels sleepy and he begins to doze, when a village woman passes by. His belly full and his mind clouded by alcohol, the beggar no longer wants to eat and drink, but as soon as he sees the woman he satisfies his lust. This is a story written by Guy de Maupassant. I have not read it. The man who told me the story told me about his keen interest in the subject. Yes, no doubt, it is interesting. But all the interest is in the rude manner of describing the Truth, according to which a human being who moves from one situation to another behaves in a certain way in accordance with each situation. However, the interest that it presents differs from that of the story of the dumb person I told you just now. The Truth is not simply highlighted as before; it also destroys the other ideals. Because one does not forget the ideal which has been destroyed, the interest one could derive from this story disappears because of the destruction of the ideal and the work becomes ineffective, and also it is very possible that serious harm may result from several repetitions of the story, I think. Under these circumstances, commitments of extraction cannot be made. And since commitments cannot be made, rather than say that these works have no existence of their own, it would be preferable, in my opinion, to state that similar works should not be allowed to exist. The ordinary world becomes depraved, and the more that moral awareness is diluted, the more the moral ideal becomes demeaned. In short, as the moral sense of ordinary people becomes progressively dulled, writers and critics begin to focus on other ideals and the high ideals disappear. In the end, we may wonder whether a state of mind has developed in which Good, for example, is considered not very important while Truth above all should be shown. If contemporary Japan is such a society, we cannot do anything about it; but, if we admit that Western society is becoming depraved in the same way and that the ideal of arts and letters is directed only towards Truth, to adopt such ideas immediately, without reflecting on the reasons why Western society is spreading them, and to import them from Kobe or Yokohama, would be to act very hastily. I think that, when we have imported the plague from abroad, since ancient times the people who have rejoiced have not been numerous. When I say such things, I feel I am using extravagant terms but, in fact, when I see works written by foreigners, as the rules of extraction do not work very well for us, I sometimes find them disagreeable and I cannot help it.

It is not necessarily a question of contemporary work: the play *Othello*[24] by Shakespeare provides a good illustration of the

---

[24] *Othello or the Moor of Venice*, a play in five acts by Shakespeare, written in 1604. A Moorish general in the service of Venice, Othello married the beautiful and virtuous Desdemona.

phenomenon I have spoken about. I think that the development of the action and the description of the characters contain Truth. I had occasion to give a lesson on this subject two or three times, and I understand the point of view perfectly. However, after reading this play, I am left with a very unpleasant feeling. I have no impression of anything pathetic or chivalrous. I experience only a strange feeling. If I had the time, I would analyze my reaction fully and submit the results to you, but as I am not in the mood, I shall say in summary that it is an unpleasant work. Although there are many Shakespearean critics, it is strange in my opinion that none of them has commented on this. In the last analysis, I suppose that it is attributable to the fact that we are talking about a work which uses the ideal of Truth as its sole criterion of judgment. As far as contemporary writings are concerned, well, I do not think that I have the time to list all those that are affected by this malaise. The woman known as Hedda Gabler,[25] even though she lacks nothing, deceives people, causes suffering, mocks them and plunges them into affliction. From the beginning to the end, she is an unpleasant woman. The person who depicted this unpleasant woman is the famous Ibsen. A minor government official had a vain wife.[26] He obtained from an acquaintance an invitation for him and his wife to attend a party given by a minister. He thought she would quite simply be content to enjoy it, but things turned out differently. His wife acted like a spoilt child; she went on and on and quibbled over her dress or what hairpin she should wear. On this occasion, the husband found the

---

[25] This play by Henrik Ibsen (1828–1906) tells the story of a beautiful young aristocrat desperate to escape from her husband and her stifling world.

[26] These are the two protagonists of the Maupassant story, "The Necklace," published in 1884. The wife of a minor official in the Ministry of National Education shines one evening at a Ministry ball. She loses a diamond necklace there which was borrowed for the occasion, and to pay for it she has to spend the rest of her life in poverty.

means, unwisely, to obtain money and gave in to the will of his wife. When the moment arrived when they were to go to the party, his wife again became obstinate. At the last minute, she stubbornly insisted to him that if she was not wearing precious stones, such as diamonds or rubies, it would be impossible for her to go to the party. The husband was once more embarrassed by the demands of his wife, but he came up with a plan. As it would only be for one party, his wife would borrow a precious diamond necklace from a friend who by chance possessed one. The plan was fulfilled in record time. The wife, on the evening of the party, in an excess of joy and excitement, danced, skipped, flew and laughed, and finally dropped part of the precious borrowed object on the floor. The couple turned white, knowing that it was the wife's fault for skipping around too much. But even though she moderated her skipping from then on, the diamonds did not reappear. As a result, after consulting each other, they were forced to borrow money on unreasonable terms. Then, scouring all quarters of Paris, they eventually found a diamond necklace that seemed identical to the borrowed one. Without exceeding the period of the loan, the wife went to her friend and returned the jewels without saying anything about the loss. At the time, the problem was resolved without difficulty. However, the repayment of the debt was not a simple matter. As the custom in Paris is to return what has been borrowed, despite her former haughtiness the wife, reduced to such an extremity, abruptly altered her behavior and went to work in kitchens, preparing meals and carrying out all sorts of tasks, and getting chilblains and living off potatoes. After several years, she was able to repay the loan completely. But by then, like any woman who has been a maid of all work, she had a strange face, strange hands and rough clothes. The story has one more chapter.

19. The Ideal of the Contemporary Man of Letters (4): The Predominance Accorded to the Ideal of Truth

One day, the wife, carrying a bamboo basket or something similar, left the house to buy Western tofu and unexpectedly met the woman who had lent her the diamond necklace some years before. This lady radiated elegance and the wife, who now looked like a maid, was somewhat ashamed to greet her. However, she walked resolutely towards her and began a conversation: "Oh, how seldom we meet!" But, as she expected, the other lady had forgotten what had happened so long ago and became defensive, pointing out very clearly that this maid was not someone she knew. Without being discouraged, the wife launched into explanations: "To repay the cost of your diamond necklace, I have had to do crazy things and live under a curse. It's still the same now!" When she described the details of the matter, the woman replied laughing, "But the diamonds were fake!" This is the end of the story. This is a work of Maupassant, whom I have already mentioned. The last sentence is extremely original and I think that it is one of the writer's most successful passages. Real aspects of Parisian society are minutely scrutinized and we are perhaps inclined to applaud and say that it is well described and very successful. It is there that the ideal of this work lies, and it is there that the unpleasantness lies. As it is a question of circumstances that the wife cannot escape, she overcomes her vanity and is able to abase herself to become like an uncouth woman brought up in the country. The action of repaying this debt at the end of several years of hard work, completely against her nature, denotes a remarkable intention and behavior. If there had been in Guy de Maupassant any feeling of moral compassion for his character, he would have at least been able to make better use of the wife's mental disposition. No account is taken in any way of the heroine's honesty, put into practice at the price of so much effort. I think the word "positive" would be a little exaggerated. However, as this

woman has been indirectly deceived by another and has under-
taken mundane work for no reason, when everything would
have gone well for her even if she had done nothing, her honest application cannot receive any reward from Maupassant or
from the reader, either on the spiritual or on the material level.
As even showing compassion might appear stupid, one does not
show any. The reason for this comes in the last sentence. The
writer has here created an inconsistent conclusion that has a
singular effect. By means of this last sentence, Maupassant, taking advantage of the moral sense of the reader, prevents him
from feeling compassion towards an individual who would
seem completely to deserve it. On the one hand, this work
depicts a good action, which could arouse compassion; on the
other hand, even though it implies that we must feel compassion, it prevents us from doing so. Even if there is a profound
examination of people's actions, as soon as one undermines the
ideal of Good in such a way, it is impossible for me to approve
the procedure. I would like to give you yet another example. It
is now the turn of Zola. An old man has a wife much younger
than himself. The wedding took place in the normal way, but
for unknown reasons it is impossible for them to have children.
The old man is worried about this situation and consults a doctor. As doctors have a duty to find a solution to every problem,
the doctor gives him the following curious advice: "Well, if you
go to the seaside and you eat the shellfish called X, then you
should be able to have children."

The old man, full of joy, immediately goes with his wife to
a very well-known seaside bathing station. At this point, a man
staying at the resort, feeling a compatibility with the woman,
first on an age level and then in other ways, too, quickly makes
friends with her—although she limits herself to the behavior
appropriate to a married woman. Each day the two young people dive into the sea and swim together. On the beach the old
man watches them from afar. He says to himself, "These young

people are really full of energy!" And in his heart of hearts, he conceives a secret admiration for them. One day they go for a walk on the shore. Because of his advanced age, the husband, detesting beaches with too many pebbles, walks along the sea wall. The two young people walk briskly and fearlessly on the wave-swept shore. After covering five or six hundred meters, they enter a cave on the edge of the shore. We cannot say whether it is lucky or unlucky, but as the tide comes in, it becomes difficult for them to leave. The old man, sitting above the cave, contemplates the white sails on the open sea as he waits for the tide to go out so that the two young people can leave the cave. As he becomes bored, he suddenly remembers the doctor's advice and picks out the recommended shellfish. He eats some and then, while he waits, he eats some more. Finally, before the tide has receded and the two young people have come out of the cave, he has eaten a large quantity of the shellfish. The adventure ends at this point. He goes back home with his wife and has a go. In the blink of an eye, the effectiveness of the seafood is felt and his wife becomes pregnant the following month. They do not know whether it will be a lovely boy or a girl, but the fact that his wife is bringing a child into the world fills the old man with satisfaction. And this feeling is the end of the story. I do not know what Zola was thinking when he published this work. But in my opinion, even more than in the Maupassant story, if the ideal that progresses one step in a certain direction were absent, the work would be completely unfinished. When we go to a Yose show where there are often people from the lower classes, it sometimes happens that they applaud strange passages—for it is strange that one should applaud only at times when ordinary people frown. If this Zola came to Japan and honored a Yose hall with his presence, he would doubtless be able, in my opinion, to catch a crowd of spectators in his net.

20. The Ideal of the Contemporary Man of Letters (5): Morbid Phenomena. The Meaning of Truth in Arts and Letters

Obviously I am not saying that contemporary literature is completely infected by this evil. However, I think that the trend exists in several places. There is no doubt about it. This trend, which is manifested in the form of morbid phenomena, comes from the fact that we attach too much importance to this ideogram called Truth. Gentlemen, if we take a secret policeman as an example, I do not think that he would be fit company. This policeman, when he goes home, returns to his wife and children. In his relationships with his neighbors, he behaves as a normal person. He is in no way an animal without moral sense. He perhaps shows refinement to a point when he glances, with no intention of buying, at a rolled-up painting on a nightstand, or even lets himself go to gaze at a bonsai. But the secret policeman, since he exercises the duties of a secret policeman, apart from the fact of grasping the truth of things, has no regard for anyone. It would be an exaggeration to say that he "shows Truth in broad daylight." However, if we consider the duties inherent to his function, using the term in a basic sense, we can go so far as to say that he is searching for "Truth." Therefore, if we consider this individual purely in relation to the duties that he exercises, well, he does not seem like a normal human being. He has no morals or sense of Beauty. It goes without saying that the sense of the Sublime is also lacking in him. And however much he may be beautiful on the physical level, comparing him in any way with Good or a noble situation, it is impossible to feel the least emotion towards him. I have no wish to become a secret policeman. The reason why certain people exercise such duties is because that they are completely lacking in three ideals out of the four. And the lowest aspect of the last ideal makes the policeman act inconsiderately. Such beings clearly cannot be human. In some circumstances we would be better off with machines. And as these machines would be efficient, they could render enormous service to the police headquarters that would give them a salary and would care for them as if they were well-behaved animals. However, as their professional occupation consists of doing work more appropriate to machines, these people lose the privilege of being considered as human beings while they fulfill their duties and show irreverence towards normal human beings. If we take contemporary men of letters and compare them to secret policemen (please forgive me this grave impoliteness), if they are proud and publish in broad daylight works that profess the word "Truth," whose real purpose is to mock other ideals, these writers, who one will take as individuals, leaving on one side the writer, must in all probability be people who lack something. Here we must talk in a morbid fashion. I have already said that the ideals that derive from the four different categories are of equal weight and must not overlap each other. If this principle of equality between the different ideals is not satisfied, difficulties can occur. There are clearly a certain number of overlaps. In these circumstances, a person who is seen to go beyond his particular territory must have a sufficiently broad vision to frighten those who overlap their domain. On this point Othello is, as I have said, the easiest to defend. As to the examples taken from Maupassant and Zola, these produce an impression of crudeness and baseness that recalls what one feels about the secret police.

I have repeatedly stressed that there are four different forms of ideals, and I have also said that these four ideals are different from each other in various ways. These four ideals are the ones that are shown by artists, but in a sense they are also the ideals of people in general; and the artist or the man of letters, who possesses the highest of these four ideals is at the same time an individual who possesses the highest and the broadest ideal. And only by possessing the highest and broadest ideal as an individual human being is it possible for him to exercise an influence on others. Thus, arts and letters are not simply a question of technique for him. As for works by writers who do not have this quality of personality, they will express only a common ideal or no ideal at all, and the energy that determines what impact authors have on their environment will certainly be weakened. When we use a particular technique to deploy a powerful personality and to cause it to shine, the effect of arts and letters spreads its profound brightness with clarity for eternity. When I say that it spreads its brightness, I do not mean at all that the name of the writer will be passed from generation to generation, or that he will unleash tumultuous forces on the general public. The strong personality of the writer impregnates the heart and mind of the reader, spectator and listener, becomes flesh and blood for them, and is passed on to posterity. This is how I understand the expression. If people who dedicate themselves to arts and letters are not passed on to posterity in the way I have indicated, the fact itself of being passed on does not confer any advantage. We are not talking about being passed on to posterity in the form of two or three lines in a dictionary of proper names, nor of the memory of an individual himself in posterity. It is simply the written word that is transmitted. If, in the strict sense of the word, the writer's Ego is passed on to the following generation, then to other generations, we are aware only that this is an incentive to dedicate oneself to arts and letters. We are aware only of a reality in which an Ego is not an isolated entity but forms an intrinsic part of the general spirit of society. We simply understand that arts and letters have relationships, which occur according to circumstances, with popular conceptions of morality. As we start from this irresistible desire to live and maintain the ideal of differentiation, he who achieves this ideal by any means accomplishes a worthy deed that extends and elevates the purpose of our existence. He who best achieves the most grandiose ideal does something that allows the purpose of our existence to be achieved in the best possible manner. Because of this, a master of art and letters is never a man with nothing to do. Even Basho,[27] who wrote negative haiku, or Rihaku,[28] who composed licentious poems, were in no way men with nothing to do. Even if we compare them to a high government official or a powerful family, these men of letters or artists live a very meaningful existence and all, in their way, contribute to the great purpose of human life.

21. Discussion on the Various Techniques (1)

When we talk about an ideal, we are not talking about just anything. However we live out our life, we must complete an examination paper that deals with life's problems in the best possible way. A painting by an artist, a book by a writer, these are examination papers. When the man of letters or the artist details the problems of the world in which he lives, using different expedients, he merely acts as a producer of examination papers which each must interpret in his own way. For an examination paper to have the power of conviction, the message must not be ambiguous. If the question is subtle and spiritual, if shadows appear, difficulties will arise and will hinder the communication of ideas or mutual understanding. What we call "techniques" are the instruments that the man of letters or artist uses to achieve maximum clarity in this examination paper. The instrument is not the substance of the work.

---

[27] Matsuo Munefusa, known as Basho, was a poet, painter and Buddhist monk. Born in Ueno in 1644, he died in Osaka in 1694. A specialist in *haikai-renga* ("free poems in a chain"), he also wrote haiku, a poem in 17 syllables and a privileged method of expression, but above all he was a master of *haibun*, poetic prose punctuated with haiku.

[28] Li Bo, Li Bai or Li Po, Rihaku in Japanese (707–762), was a Chinese poet of the Tang dynasty. Drunk, it is believed, every day of the year (over a third of his poems mentioned drink) and a tramp, he had a resolute taste for independence.

Gentlemen, it is possible that you will tell me that you have understood. It is also possible that you will tell me that you have not understood. This is for those who have understood. For those who have not understood, I must explain. I have just said that technique is an instrument. Talking generally, this is clear. But if we stand back and reflect a little, it becomes much more difficult to understand. When we hear someone asking what this technique is, it is extremely difficult to say. Ordinarily, we explain it as a procedure to express an idea. But since it is a question of an idea communicated by means of this procedure, we must not consider only the procedure, straying from the idea. Conversely, we must not, obviously, highlight the idea by moving away from the procedure. Therefore, when we carefully examine this problem, we wonder how far the procedure goes and where the ideas start. This becomes remarkably ambiguous. If I can talk for a moment about this piece of chalk, it is something that we can consider separately from the white color. When we take this piece of chalk as an extremely simplified criterion and begin to discuss it, if we omit the white color, the shape disappears completely. On the other hand, if we take away the shape, the white color disappears completely. At the same time, we can say that, while these elements are separate from each other they join together and that, when they join together, they separate from each other. This point becomes very annoying if we discuss it on a philosophical level. Therefore, so that it will be easy to understand, I am going to provide you with an example and proceed to explain it.

Recently, in one of my university classes, wishing to give such an example, I cited two quotations and I am going to use them now. The first is from Shakespeare and the second is from Daniel Defoe. If we compare them, we can clearly see a distinction on the technical level as well as in content:

"Uneasy lies the head that wears a crown."

"Kings have frequently lamented the miserable Consequences of being born to great things, and wished they had been placed in the Middle of the two Extremes, between Mean and the Great." The broad meaning of each is so clear that there is no need to explain it. Shakespeare's line tells us that crowned heads do not have a good time, and expresses the idea that people of royal extraction are afflicted by unhappiness because of their birth. The quotation from Defoe expresses the idea that kings would often prefer to have led their lives somewhere between the opposing extremes of the Mean and the Great. It goes without saying that, as a single line from the first author is quoted and it is in verse form, whilst the quotation from the second is taken from a prose novel, if we are interested in the context of the two quotations we can discuss their subject matter differently; but if we take each text in isolation and examine it from a critical point of view, extremely important differences appear on the technical level used. I will explain as follows. As regards the content of the two extracts, no one would doubt that they are not very different from each other. Therefore, at the level of ideas, I have no problem in taking them together and considering them as twins. But in spite of the fact that these two quotations are similar at the level of ideas, we are left with a totally different impression on reading them. Recently, I needed to write a critique of Daniel Defoe's work, and when I re-read the text I was reminded by chance of this quotation and I also suddenly remembered Shakespeare's phrase from *Henry V*. Despite the similarity of the content, I was very struck by the difference in the sentiments expressed. When I began to wonder why there was this difference, even going so far as to try to dissect them with a scalpel, I found that I did not understand them clearly. So, in my talk, I will now proceed to a thorough dissection of the feelings that I had at that time. When one looks at Shakespeare's opinion, he emphasizes the personal situation of a king over the years (whether it lasts ten or twenty years, it is only a question of the time for which he effectively reigns) without expressing it in words that imply a long time, but on the contrary reducing it to a single moment. We have here complete *savoir-faire*. If we express the meaning of this phrase more thoroughly, this is what comes out of it. The word "uneasy" may seem to express a vague psychological situation. However, in reality it is a very effective word and full of subtlety. It is a word that allows one to express situations in which the mind is disconcerted, as for example when one is sitting on a chair of which one foot is broken, or when one has forgotten to fasten the braces of one's trousers and they are threatening to slip or fall down. Of course, what I call a situation in which the mind is disconcerted is something that necessarily implies a development over time, but in this case the scene appears immediately in our field of vision, with no evolution over time. Therefore, the word "uneasy" expresses a situation in which, even if we are in involved in something of long duration, we shorten it to a minute, to an instant even, and the expression represents the mind instantaneously, as if it were a picture.

22. Discussion on the Various Techniques (2)

Listening to these suggestions, someone perhaps will come up unexpectedly and take me aside. He will say, "This situation that you call 'uneasy' perhaps exists, but a feeling of uneasiness on the physical level is not the same as such a feeling on the psychological level. It is probably possible to divide in terms of time a situation of physical awkwardness and its reflection in the mirror of imagination as something psychological. But in the case of uneasiness manifesting itself on a psychological level, that to say a state of anxiety or trouble, it would not, I think, be possible to reconstitute this impression in such a way!" Faced with such an attack, I would respond as follows. It is certain that such situations as we describe as uneasy exist, and it is not always necessary to imagine these cases. Even if the uneasiness felt by the king is shown at the psychological level, it is not necessary to state it in psychological terms. Rather than say that it is not necessary, it would be more appropriate to state that we are not prepared to do so. After the word "uneasy," one finds the word "lies"—that is, in bed, lying down. "Lies" is a word that is applied to the material state of things. Therefore, when we read uneasy and we are perplexed, wondering what this "uneasy" is about, the meaning of "uneasy" becomes very clear because it is immediately followed by "lies."

So, some people may then make the following criticism: "'Lies' also has a double meaning. There is, of course, the material side, but we also use this word to express something intangible. Therefore, when we hear the expression 'uneasy lies' we have the impression that what you are talking to us about is not happening." Faced with this criticism, I would articulate my defense as follows: if you say that you have not been convinced by the expression "uneasy lies," the situation will improve when you read the third word "head." This is something physical. Even if one goes so far as to take the word "head" in its allegorical sense, in reading the succession of words "uneasy lies the head," it is impossible to justify the explanation that "head" is given an abstract function, or that it means intellectual capacity. Everyone will understand that what we have here is a head appearing in physical form, a head on which hair grows. And having understood head in its real sense, "lies" also can only have one meaning. And pursuing the analysis, it would also be difficult to take "uneasy" as referring to something that cannot be seen with no relationship to physical reality. In addition, as regards this physical sense of "uneasy," although we do not know how long the uneasiness will last, even if it continues over the long term, for the whole of its duration it will always be perceptible to sight. That is the situation. And because we have a situation in which the state expressed will always be visible, even if we split up this whole into momentary fragments, viewing it in fragments shows us the totality that will be expressed over the long term.

Putting it differently, we could say that it is possible to evoke in the mind a reduction of something that has lasted ten or twenty years to a brief moment of time.

Something that reflects the line from Shakespeare occurs today. Having talked about time, I will now talk about space. Let us analyze it in detail. If we ask people whether the ideograms representing king indicate an abstract or a real word, everyone would answer, in my opinion, that it is a definite term. Good, therefore there is no doubt that it is a word with a real, physical nature. However, if we content ourselves with simply nodding agreement to this, we will have problems in gaining a clear idea. If we say that we will try to paint a portrait of the king, we will not immediately, in my opinion, be able to make even a rough sketch. We remember this being who has the name of king in the form of an untidy and fairly confused sketch in our minds. When we say "The head that wears a crown," the idea of king immediately occurs to us very clearly. When we think about this idea, it is only the physical aspect of it that is at present comprehensible. The task of obtaining a precise knowledge of each aspect of the king is fraught with ambiguity and is very difficult to achieve. It is exactly as if we look through spectacles that have not been adjusted to suit our eyesight. The fact that this object exists independently from other things is clear; but it is only its independence from other things that appears with any clarity and its content is unclear. Now when we say, "uneasy lies the head that wears a crown" we feel that the focus has been very rapidly sharpened. If we talk about a king, we should envisage him completely, as an individual. And when we try to build in our imagination a complete picture of him, the image becomes hazy. We do not know where to concentrate our imagination, as the king is made up of several parts. To avoid this haziness, therefore, Shakespeare picks out for us, among this quantity of parts, the best that one can imagine in the context. This is what he teaches us; it is not that the king has legs or hands or that he has a backbone or intestines. The part of the body which he points to, indicating the thing that allows us to see the king if we concentrate all our attention on it, is this crowned head that shines with a dazzling glare. Whilst, just now, we were suffering because we were not able to distinguish the whole in all its clarity, the fact that we have had to concentrate our attention in this way, to direct our gaze at this crowned head, has enabled us to perceive the king. It may only be this part that is clear, but as this part constitutes what substantially represents the king, when it clearly appears to us, it is as if the whole clearly appeared to us. Shakespeare, in fact, leads us to the essential feature that we must see in the person. This essential feature sheds light on the whole, and since there is no need for us to direct our attention beyond this essential central feature, the other, unnecessary features can be ignored. Shakespeare economizes the attention of the reader. If we consider his central feature in physical terms, Shakespeare reduces a tall person, who is known as King, and transforms him into a simple crowned head. A man one metre eight centimeters tall is reduced to a head less than thirty centimeters tall.

23. Discussion on the Various Techniques (3)

On close examination, Shakespeare's sentence appears to reduce both time and space, and portrays the long duration and the vast space in an arresting way. The vision is blurred, just as it is when we look at something a long way off with the naked eye, but once we have found our glasses, something that seemed enormous is reduced; it is more aesthetic and this makes a great impact. The person who actually adjusts our spectacles to suit our vision is Shakespeare. When we read this line, we are left with an impression of poetry.

However, when we read the sentence by Daniel Defoe, it is entirely different. This gentleman's style is to let himself go in long and short passages, and there is nothing than can be reduced to "sweet fire." Even though we are looking at a point a long way off, we can see it with the naked eye. It is not a question of using glasses, whether or not they are adapted to our sight. Well, we can say that it is a style characterized by clumsiness. We can also say that it is a form of writing that denotes either coldness or lack of benevolence, a form of writing that is not kind enough to be easy for its readers. And it would not be hard to see what I mean, I think, if I were to make the critical comment that this sentence, in which we find no flexibility or elasticity, is one that proceeds with heavy steps, always only on its own two legs, because of its heritage from its parents, unaware of the means of transport that have been invented, such as the steam train, the electric train or, of course, the rickshaw. As a result, we have the impression that this is prose. As regards the sentence set out here in prose, we can say that it comes at us at an average speed, with no demonstration of talent, without riding a horse or using a vehicle. It is in no way my intention to rail against this. It is fine, from time to time to go forward at a moderate pace. Now, the fact that this sentence walks and drags its feet all year as if it had wooden legs, and as if it were obeying rules that must be followed when one rushes towards a fire or attends a funeral, even if we accept that this befits the attitude of the person concerned, it really seems to me to be a story lacking in talent. Defoe had an extremely easy style of writing and wrote about three hundred works during his life. I think that he is a prose writer who is like a rickshaw puller.

On this note, I am going to end my comparative criticism of the quotations from the two writers. And if we wonder about what conclusion we can draw from this study, I would say that the techniques that we use in arts and letters are of great importance. If the techniques were lacking, the value of the ideas that suddenly come to us would not be revealed, and that would be eminently regrettable. Shakespeare and Defoe describe the same idea, but the result, as we have seen, is very different. That such a difference is manifested in spite of the nature of the idea is entirely attributable to the technique used. That is my conclusion! Recently, certain Japanese writers have stubbornly maintained that techniques are superfluous. But as I have not heard what you think about this, I shall not say anything. However, referring to the argument I have set out, as it is a question of artists and men of letters, I am convinced that there is no reason to reject techniques on the pretext of their ineffectiveness, and I am persuaded that the explanation I have submitted to you does not contain any error on the theoretical level or on any other level. If it were your intention to interpret the musical works of celebrated composers while attaching no importance to the clumsiness that you might bring to them, then perhaps techniques in literature would seem superfluous to you. However, I do not hold this opinion. And among people who consider techniques superfluous, it seems to me that there are many who say that their aim is to bring themselves into contact with this lower world, and that if they do not do so it is a stinging defeat, and that the technique they use to achieve this aim is unimportant. In this regard, too, I have heard no clear explanation up to now and I cannot clearly understand the sense of such a process. Every time I hear such suggestions, they seem to me strange. However much we may give the order to "come into contact," if the writer does not understand the nature of this objective, he will be very perplexed. However much we inconsiderately make a great racket by shouting "It is the real world here below, it is the real world here below!," since you do not explain to me what "It is the real world here below!" means, and given that for me this is like sounding an alarm when there is no fire, I remain calm. But people shout "Get out! Make room!," and we can assume that afterwards there will be serious problems. Before issuing an injunction to come into contact with the world here below, it is necessary to explain what this world here below is, and what entering into contact with it means and what the totality of this expression covers. Therefore, if I am told that techniques are superfluous, since I have not felt the need to discuss this up to now, I abstain for the present from making comments on the world here below. If you wish to know the meaning of expression "come into contact with the world here below," I can readily give you a clear reply, but as I have something to tell you in passing, please wait for another chapter.

24. Discussion on the Techniques (4): The Techniques that Comprise the Ideal

As I cannot make you wait, I shall proceed immediately to the next part. Painters, as opposed to some men of letters who stubbornly proclaim that you must come into contact with the world below, and that techniques are completely superfluous, are not like we turbulent people; they work seriously and are not going to sound the alarm except in a case of absolute emergency. If we look at how they accomplish their art, they show complete indifference as to whether one enters into contact with the world here below or not; and we note that they are keen to perfect their techniques by dedicating all their passion to them. It goes without saying that I am completely ignorant of the rules of painting, and therefore I clearly have no right to poke my nose into it. However, these layman's suggestions can perhaps serve as a reference point. As I rarely have the occasion to meet you, gentlemen, and we are discussing today arts and letters as a whole, I will say these bold words to you. Gentlemen, when you dedicate yourself to painting people, you use models; when you reproduce plants or trees, you do it from nature, either in the open air or in a studio. These working methods are perfect. This is more interesting research than that of men of letters who content themselves, on a surface of 4.5 tatamis, to aligning coldly, as they wish, unreal things, and creating in their imagination, as if they were dreaming, inappropriate beings, landscapes and affairs. You are clearly well aware of the merits of this: however much I talk, it will be like preaching to the converted. Following the usual order of lectures, I am going to tell you what I believe I understand, even if I do not really understand it properly. In this study, the main points that we first discern are in my opinion of two types. First, I believe that it is possible to be able skillfully and rapidly to discern plainly, for example, the variety of forms and colors, and of objects and beings, and to reproduce in minute detail what one has clearly grasped. Second, the lines and dots used to depict this detail make the varied forms and shades of the object or being that one is describing relatively independent and, depending on the nature of these lines and dots, a certain type of skill is in evidence. This second technique, while still a technique, allows the ideal to be shown, and, as a result, can no longer be considered as purely technique. At present, ordinary painters in Japan, for the most part, value only pure technique. In spite of this attitude, when we surrender ourselves to appreciation on the artistic level by letting ourselves be guided by the artist's whim, in the majority of cases our interest lies partly in the fact that the work reveals the personality of the painter; that is, it expresses a certain form of ideal in one way or another. For example, even in the way of drawing a line (even though the drawing is not made up of this single line), by the vigor contained therein, one can identify the ideal that underlies the painter's intention. The state of a curved line can portray the ideal of Beauty. Lines that are clear and distinctly broad or narrow can imply an intellectual meaning. Or, indeed, it is possible to accumulate charming perceptions and sweet sentiments. (It is inescapable that the fact that the ideals of Intelligence and Beauty are not equally manifest is inherent in the nature of the work.) This reveals that these lines and dots alone encompass the ideal. And we may think that we can thus deduce that we are capable of understanding the human personality when we look at something that has been written, as in ideograms making up an epitaph or a lithograph of a written text, and that the technique (according to an extent to the culture and training of the person) includes the ideal. However, the technique that we have just described, that is to say, the skill in conveying a clear perception of the object or being, is completely alien to the ideal and is independent of the technique we are now discussing. To explain this in a way that is easy to understand, well, the nuances of intelligence, perception and will do not manifest themselves when one produces, in painting or describing an object or being, something that resembles the original. There is an absence of liveliness; something mechanical comes into play, without our knowing why. The technique I am talking about is truly that: I am criticizing here people who cherish the hope of becoming artists while possessing only this technique. It goes without saying, gentlemen, that you in no way think that the possession of this technique alone is sufficient to make an artist. However, while we superimpose technique and research, can we not say that we are sometimes induced to make this error despite ourselves? If I return again to the preceding chapter and to what I call "fundamentals," as I said before, arts and letters express an ideal through the depiction of a being or a perceptible object and, therefore, if I give this aim prime significance and a certain form of ideal is not revealed by the perceptible object, its existence becomes colorless. I think technique draws its merit from being, first of all, a skilful method that allows an ideal to become perceptible. If we want to give a name to those technicians lacking in ideals, well, we can, in my opinion, refer to them as common artists keen to exhibit their technique. If we say that such artists are common, this is because they express no ideal. Or, even if an ideal is expressed, because of its futility, its insignificant scale and its banality, it can in no way be allowed to come into contact with the world here below.

25. The Artist or Man of Letters: A Reducing Influence

In borrowing an expression that has been popular for a little while, I said that it was not possible to come into contact with the world here below. I think that the meaning of "the world here below" is more or less understood in light of our discussion just now. However, as I promised, I will proceed clearly with appropriate simplicity by offering a formal explanation—or, at least, so it will seem to me. We all hope that a succession of awareness will result. This procedure, and the modification of the content of awareness that occurs, will provide us with a field of choice. This subject gives us an ideal, and for me, coming into contact with the world here below means realizing this ideal. Outside this context, even if we wanted to come into contact with the world here below it would not be possible. And since there are four ideals—Truth, Beauty, Good and the Sublime—people who are capable of realizing one of these four ideals are those who are able to understand the world to the necessary degree. Someone who can reveal the ideal of Truth and another who is capable of expressing the ideal of Beauty come into contact with the world here below with the same rights and significance. Those who can reveal the ideal of Good and those who know how to present the ideal of the Sublime can come into contact with the world here below with the same rights and significance. Whatever ideal they reveal, they all come into contact with the world in the same way. Suggesting that only one of these four ideals can come into contact with the world here below and that the others cannot, contrary to what has been demonstrated at the theoretical level, is boastful and arrogant and does not lead to any valid conclusion. Truth is an ideal that can expand and become more profound. However, to say that Truth is the only ideal that can enable us to make true contact with the world here below and that other ideals are powerless is to adopt the position of the "colorblind" who recognize no other way in the world than Truth. The four cardinal ideals can each authorize our passage and, if we can use the term "precious," well, they are all four very precious.

The four ideals are subject to differentiation and so metamorphoses occur. The opportunities for developing these metamorphoses have increased. The man who has realized the newest ideal in these metamorphoses is the one who finds a new significance in coming into the world below. The man who has realized in these metamorphoses the most profound ideal is the one who has come into contact with the world here below. (It is not worth the trouble of saying that "profound" is an adjective which describes the four ideals of Truth, Good, Beauty and the Sublime. Such declarations as "It is profound because black misery reigns!" or "It is profound because melancholy permeates it," have no other meaning.) The man who has realized in these metamorphoses the broadest ideal is the one who has come into wide-ranging contact with the world here below. The man who, combining these ideals, achieves them by using a perfect technique, is the one we call "the ideal artist," a Saint of arts and letters. There is nothing unusual in the notion of a Saint: it simply allows us to approach in a certain way the problem of whether we must live.

When an advanced ideal is combined with a perfect technique, artistic and literary works attain ideal perfection. (It is therefore completely logical that the ideal perfection of the man of letters or artist changes from period to period.) When the artist or the man of letters attains perfection, people who have relationships with him experience a reducing influence when opportunity offers them the possibility to come into contact with him. This phenomenon of the reducing influence derives from the supreme influence that the artist or the man of letters can exercise over us. My expression "when opportunity offers them the possibility…" refers to the case when the ideal that has appeared in these arts and letters, reaching perfection, is combined with the ideal of our own Ego, or even the case when the ideal of our own Ego, fascinated by the ideal of arts and letters, attains perfect truth, either in novelty or in profundity, at the time it sees the Light. We say that people who do not enjoy the beneficence of Buddha are difficult to save, but fine words do not appear only in Buddhism. People who possess a different quality of ideal, even if someone wishes to exercise an influence over them, or if they want themselves to experience such an influence, cannot achieve this, no matter what they do.

As the ideograms that signify "reducing influence" are rather strange, I suspect that you do not understand them properly. If I explain them to you, the following meaning will emerge: given that the artist or the man of letters expresses with the aid of words or colors the ideal that his Ego has created, the ideal thus formed comprises what his particular variety of awareness has reproduced—that is, something that constitutes a certain continuity. Thus, in this context, the meaning contained in the expression "reaching the limits of pleasure" relates to the continuity of awareness manifested by the artist. If our own continuity of awareness must be mad to correspond to a certain degree with that of the artist, then, what we call "pleasure" must not occur. What I call a "reducing influence," is a phenomenon that is produced only through the realization of this correspondence.

26. The Two Varieties of Reducing Influence

To all appearances, the meaning of this "correspondence" is clear. The continuity of awareness resulting from a correspondence between that of the artist and our own, which fills our hearts and leaves traces in us even after we have finished a literary work, is what I call "the phenomenon of reducing influence." I must just therefore explain the Chinese characters that comprise the term "reduction." These relate to the term "correspondence": when we talk about correspondence, we mean that my and another's awareness mingle and become one. But we must refer back to the time before the correspondence has taken place, because once correspondence has taken place there are no longer two separate awarenesses. If we penetrate into these regions, having already detached ourselves from the situation of the common people, we transcend the framework within which the Ego and other beings or objects are situated. Now, transcending this limit between the Ego and external beings or objects is the starting point of my lecture, and constitutes the fundamental origin of all this speculation. As a result, while we continue to benefit subconsciously from artistic and literary works in forgetting our Ego and forgetting that of the artist or the writer (this implies a process that is not directed towards introspection), there is neither time nor space but only continuity of awareness. However, what I want to say is that, because there is no time or space, this does not mean that there is none in the work; it means, rather, that the time that opposes the Ego to the work and the space that the Ego occupies do not exist; and it is just as if, while reading, we are not aware of time passing and have forgotten where we are—office, home, the streets of Tokyo or bed. It is normally impossible to forget these things, since at certain moments we are in correspondence with the continuity of awareness of the writer and at others we are detached from it, because the Ego always remains the Ego and the writer or artist always remains himself. As it is the case that, when we are in this state of correspondence, we rapidly return to ourselves if a flea bites us or if the clock strikes, it is impossible to enjoy a total correspondence at will, without interruption. And thus, while the awareness of our Ego and that of the artist ceaselessly separate and conjoin, either while reading or while looking at a painting, it is impossible to attain a state of what we might call purity and simplicity. Because of this, we are usually disturbed, we start to dawdle, we become distracted. There are those who, for the whole of their life, do not once manage to cross the frontiers of impersonality to idle in a state of ecstasy. We commonly refer to them as the slaves of things.

When such people, by dint of some mysterious affinity, suddenly experience this reducing correspondence, they rejoice in the same way as a frighteningly ugly man rejoices at becoming the object of the reckless love of a woman of great beauty.

When the ideal is manifested, by favoring the continuity aspect of "the continuity of awareness" that I mentioned just now, it is generally a question of a literary work. When the ideal is manifested by favoring the content of awareness itself, a painting can be achieved. From this we can see that the ideal proceeding from the first principle (the creation of a work of literature) is revealed via a process of modification of awareness. As a result, literary works that develop on the ideal level by obeying the laws of change enable readers to experience the reducing influence easily. I call this process "the reducing influence of movement." Following on from this, the ideal proceeding from the second principle (the creation of a painting) is principally manifested in the manner of a stasis in the development of awareness. Thus, when we ingeniously use the available mechanisms to cause such a stasis, when we capture a short interval of time and use it to fulfill our objective, the person who contemplates the resulting painting can readily experience its reducing influence. I call this process "the reducing influence of serenity." However, although I have distinguished between literature and painting on the level of their fundamental creation, it is impossible really to separate them completely. And if I apply for the moment these two influences to literary analysis, we can identify a problem, which we ought to discuss, concerning the laws of movement (which we see as a dynamic principle of literature) and we are obliged to consider the appropriateness of the stasis in the development of awareness in the literary context. To date, critical theory has made no progress in this respect and, as no one is currently addressing these two problems, there is plenty of scope for research. In my "Studies on Literature," which is not yet complete, I set out my thoughts on this subject, and I therefore ask you please to refer to it. If there are people who wish, on the basis of our discussion, to acquire new knowledge to make up for my omissions and to correct my powers of diagnosis, well, it is not impossible in my opinion that critical theory may in future include the field of awareness. As I reflect generally on the appropriate procedures for creation in any given situation, I cannot say what would be the fruits of my continuing to concentrate on this aspect, but if a pioneering man of wisdom and integrity were to direct all his energy towards it, I am sure that academic circles would greatly profit from his endeavors.

27. Conclusions

I should like to add a word in conclusion. By our nature we cherish a common desire to live, whatever the cost. Because of this common motivation, there is a differentiation between the Ego and the beings or objects outside it. In this context, there arises a desire for choice as to the type of continuity of awareness to be developed; as a result of the broadening of this choice, a form of ideal is engendered. This has various ramifications which lead us to become philosophers, scientists, artists, men of letters, or even men of action. The artist or man of letters is faced with four forms of ideals and for each one he develops the continuity of awareness he desires. Briefly, we are all in some way driven by the essential challenge of the need to live. Therefore, nothing that we do is entirely devoid of practical advantage. In this lower world, we call artists or literary men "lazy" and we think they are people who spend their time doing useless things. In truth, apart from artists or men of letters, there are as many people as you can think of who do superfluous things. Among the people who fly through the town in rickshaws like arrows there are many—I do not know how many—who do useless things, more so than men of letters or artists. People who boast, for example, that they alone have skills valuable to the country are completely useless, however much *gravitas* they may assume and however much they may behave as if they alone had as much power as ten other people. As it is simply childish to ask about the meaning of usefulness or the uselessness of these gentlemen, let us reject this superfluity. If this makes them angry, let them be so. But however red they grow with anger, it will not help them. As they do not understand the reasons for what I say, they become angry. Rather than getting cross, in my opinion, they should listen with downcast eyes to my reasoning. If these men are kind enough to come and listen to me, I will always be ready to provide them with explanations. If I say that, having fulfilled my duties at the university, I do nothing but doze, snoring on the veranda, well, my friends will all laugh. Or perhaps they will not laugh but will envy my situation. Okay, I am having a doze! But I do more than doze. I have a lie-in and I go to bed early. But if I imagine, while I sleep, how to accomplish honorable ideals, I am perhaps more distinguished than someone whose talents are useful to the nation and who speeds around in a rickshaw for 26 hours at a stretch, competing with the tram. I not only sleep, but I go to sleep thinking that I am going to reflect on something important. Unfortunately, I have not elaborated on this, but in any case I am not at all a lazy person. Neither are you, gentlemen, you are not in any way lazy. People who we consider lazy are really lazy, and if they are not lazy they are idiots. Perhaps for the artist or the man of letters, free time is a necessity. However, we are not lazy. When we talk about lazy people, we mean people who are unable to make any contribution to society. A lazy person is someone who is incapable of giving his own response to the question of how we should live and who is also incapable of teaching people about the awareness of existence. Such an individual, even if he works himself out of breath, is a lazy person whereas an artist or a man of letters, however much he may doze on his veranda, is not lazy. It is out of the question to juxtapose the free time of an artist or a man of letters with that of an idle noble or a rich ne'er-do-well. Therefore, when an artist or a man of letters thinks he is a lazy person, he must ask forgiveness from God because he has abandoned his mission. The artist must resolve to show that he is not at all lazy. We must ensure an in-depth inquiry to establish that the artist or man of letters is not a lazy person in spite of all the dozing he does on his veranda. To make the audacious claim that, for this simple reason, the artist or the man of letters is not a lazy person, we must be sufficiently convinced by our reasoning. To put it another way, we must formulate our own interpretation of the way we must live and have sufficient confidence in it to make the following contentions: "Whatever people may say, since my ideal is much higher than theirs, I will not give an inch and I will not be astonished. So, keep quiet! Do not utter such pretentious words, since you know nothing about the meaning of life, or its ideal!" If it is impossible for us to adopt this attitude with confidence, however much we may use a particular technique our writing will lack quality. If we approach our writing in that way, people will make fun of us and if we say something in that spirit we will be reprimanded. We will take up our brush trembling with fear, faults will show clearly in our work, and people will say, "This lad has no strength of character yet and his ideal is immature." As a result, we will be faint-hearted and whatever our technique, it will be impossible for us to persuade people. Thus, the manifestation of influence will become hypothetical and the reducing influence will be merely hypothetical. And we will call such an artist or man of letters a lazy person. What Masaki calls "the common mind avid to exhibit its technique," well, that is perfectly appropriate for such an artist or man of letters. Briefly, what is essential to us is the ideal. The ideal is not something that is inevitably present in a literary composition or a painting. The ideal is embedded in the human being who holds it. Thus, the expression of an ideal through the power of technique is in effect an expression of part of the human personality. However much we may write, if we produce words that are not rooted in our personality, as if we are skating over a smooth surface, connecting the words just to make sentences, we are only lazy people. In the same way, however much we may do something that is "not in our line," even if we try hard and are not lazy, it will be best to abstain and save our energy. Only a man with a new deep or broad vision will find that technique is of inestimable value in helping him to bring it to this lower world. When the ordinariness of the world hinders our progress, there is no alternative but to express our ideal in an artistic or literary form through the intermediary of technique. If, through the continuity of awareness which we have discussed, a correspondence is established between our work and one person in a hundred, or even one person in a thousand, and if we have made a small contribution to the enhancement of Truth, Good, Beauty and the Sublime, which will illuminate the essence of our work like flashes of lightning, we will leave traces difficult to efface. If, progressing even further, we are able to attain the ecstasy that produces the reducing influence— because the spiritual power of arts and letters can exercise a great and intangible influence on society—we will have fulfilled our mission by obtaining eternal life in the human story.

Titles by Sōseki Natsume

Inside My Glass Doors
Translated by Sammy I. Tsunematsu
ISBN 0-8048-3312-5

Originally published in daily serialization in the *Asahi* newspaper in 1915, *Inside My Glass Doors* is a collection of thirty-nine autobiographical essays penned a year before the author's death in 1916, written in the genre of *shōhin* ("little items"), which provide a kaleidoscopic view of Sōseki's private world.

The 210th Day
Translated by Sammy I. Tsunematsu
ISBN 0-8048-3320-6
The 210th Day, first published in 1906, is written almost entirely in dialog form. It focuses on two friends, Kei and Roku, and their behavior and reactions, as they attempt to climb the rumbling Mount Aso as it threatens to erupt.

Spring Miscellany and London Essays
Translated by Sammy I. Tsunematsu
ISBN 0-8048-3326-5

First published in serial form in 1909, *Spring Miscellany* is an eclectic pastiche—a literary miscellany—of twenty-five sketches, heir to the great *zuihitsu* tradition of discursive prose, including scattered episodes from Sōseki's youth and the more recent past. Of particular interest are the accounts of his stay in England between 1900 and 1902, as well as letters he wrote at the time.

The Wayfarer

Translated by Beongcheon Yu

ISBN 4-8053-0204-6

Written in the years 1912–13, *The Wayfarer* explores the moral dilemma of individuals caught in the violent transition of Japan from feudal to modern society. The protagonist Ichiro is caught in a triangle with his wife Onao and his brother Jiro. What ensues is, in a sense, a battle of the sexes between a couple forced to live together by tradition. Ichiro's plight is that of modern man in isolation from his family, society and culture.

Grass on the Wayside

Translated by Edwin McClellan

ISBN 4-8053-0258-5

Completed in 1915 during a period of rapidly declining health, *Grass on the Wayside* is Sōseki's only autobiographical novel and the first book of its kind to appear in modern Japan. It is the story of Kenzo, Sōseki's alter ego, an unhappy, self-centered man, but one of the most fully developed characters in Japanese fiction. The book is remarkable for the depth and liveliness of its supporting characters.

The Three-Cornered World

Translated by Alan Turney

ISBN 4-8053-0201-1

In *The Three-Cornered World*, an artist leaves city life to wander in the mountains on a quest to stimulate his artistic endeavors. When he finds himself staying at an almost deserted inn, he becomes obsessed with the beautiful and strange daughter of the innkeeper, who is rumored to have abandoned her husband and fallen in love with a priest at a nearby temple. Whilst painting her, his daily conversations with the villagers provide clues to the enigma of the innkeeper's daughter.

Mon

Translated by Francis Mathy
ISBN 4-8053-0291-7

Mon is an intimate story of the consequences of an impulsive marriage, keenly portrayed in the daily life of a young couple and the quiet frustration, isolation and helplessness they face as they live a lonely and frugal life alienated from friends and relatives.

Kokoro

Translated by Edwin McClellan
ISBN 4-8053-0161-9

Written in 1914, *Kokoro* provides a timeless psychological analysis of a man's alienation from society. It tells the story of a solitary and intensely torn scholar during the Meiji era and his chance encounter on the beaches of Kamakura with a young student, who gradually learns the reasons for the scholar's aloofness and withdrawal from the world.

The Heredity of Taste

Translated by Sammy I. Tsunematsu
ISBN 4-8053-0766-8

Written in eight days, in December 1905, *The Heredity of Taste* is Sōseki's only anti-war work. Chronicling the mourning process of a narrator haunted by a friend's death, the story reveals Sōseki's attitude to the atrocity of war, specifically to the Russo-Japanese War of 1904–5, and to the personal tragedies and loss of individuality of young soldiers, and the sacrifices made by both the living and the dead.